The Suburbanization of
Multifamily Housing

The Suburbanization of Multifamily Housing

Robert Schafer
Harvard University

Lexington Books
D.C. Heath and Company
Lexington, Massachusetts
Toronto　　　London

Library of Congress Cataloging in Publication Data

Schafer, Robert.
  The suburbanization of multifamily housing.

  Includes bibliographical references.
  1. Apartment houses—United States. 2. Suburbs—United States. I. Title.
HD7287.6.U5S3   301.36'2   74-11240
ISBN 0-669-93674-x

Published simultaneously in Canada.

Printed in the United States of America.

International Standard Book Number: 0-669-93674-x

Library of Congress Catalog Card Number: 74-11240

Contents

List of Figures

List of Tables

Acknowledgments

Many individuals have provided suggestions and guidance during the course of this research. My largest debts are to John F. Kain, who has given valuable direction since the inception of the project, and Gregory K. Ingram who has been very helpful in the last stages of development. I have also benefited from discussions with William C. Apgar, Jr. and H. James Brown. I am particularly grateful to Penelope H. Schafer, my wife, for her constant support.

David Taylor of the Greater Boston Rental Housing Association was instrumental in gathering the data employed in Chapters 5, 6, 7, and 8. I am grateful to him and to the individual businessmen (who remain unnamed because of pledges of confidentiality) for their cooperation. I am also indebted to Carl Steinitz for assistance in obtaining the aid of the Rental Housing Association. I am also grateful to William Holshouser, Charles Kalauskas, and Jean MacMillan for assistance in gathering the information used in Chapters 5, 6, 7, and 8, and to Sara Jane Woodward for technical assistance in the preparation of the manuscript.

This research was financed by the Ford Foundation Grant for Urban Studies to Harvard University. Financial support was also received from the Prize Fellowship program at Harvard University.

None of these individuals or organizations is responsible for any remaining errors of commission or omission.

The Suburbanization of Multifamily Housing

1

Multifamily Housing: An Historical Perspective

The year 1957 marks the beginning of a new period in the history of residential construction in the United States. Over the next fifteen years, multifamily housing construction became a large factor in the housing market. Changes in the demand for housing were the principal reason for the increased profitability of multifamily housing construction. The major demand factors were an increase in the types of households that have traditionally demanded apartments (young singles and childless couples) and the suburbanization of employment and population. On the supply side, the rising cost of land led to its more intensive use through the construction of multiple dwelling buildings.

In the period since 1957, multifamily housing (structures with three or more units) has accounted for a growing share of private nonfarm housing starts. In 1967 private multifamily housing starts reached an unprecedented 42 percent of starts excluding mobile homes, and 32 percent of starts including mobile homes. Not since the 1920s has multifamily housing accounted for such a substantial share of new residential construction. Private multifamily housing starts as a percentage of private nonfarm housing starts over the 1900-71 period are depicted in Figure 1-1. For the first seventeen years, the fraction fluctuated around 19 percent with perhaps a slight upward trend. In 1918-20, there was an abrupt drop to nearly one-half its prior value, followed by a continual rise until 1928. Multifamily starts in 1927 and 1928 accounted for 31.7 percent of total starts. With the advent of the depression, multifamily's share of starts dropped very sharply to 6.7 percent. There was a slight rise in the 1930s, followed by a decline in 1939-42. A sharp rise occurred in 1943, followed by a decline to 4.5 percent in 1945—its lowest value in this century. Except for an increase during 1948-50, the fraction seemed to level off at about 6 percent for the next seven years. Then in 1957 the share began a rather steady climb to its current values of more than 40 percent.

The sources of housing demand and the market mechanisms of adjusting supply to demand provide the framework for understanding the shifts in multifamily's share of starts over the last seventy years. In the next section, some general aspects of demand and supply are discussed. Since multifamily housing is usually renter-occupied, the characteristics of renter households are used to analyze the demand for multifamily housing. In the remainder of the chapter, it is shown that the urbanization of the population, rising real incomes, suburbanization, and changes in the age distribution of the population were the major factors underlying the shifts in multifamily housing starts that are depicted in Figure 1-1.

1

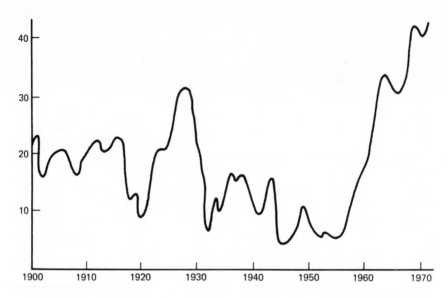

Figure 1-1. Private Multifamily (Three or More Units per Structure) as a Percentage of Private Nonfarm Housing Starts: 1900-1971. Source: Appendix A.

Demand and Supply

Population growth and household formation are basic determinants of aggregate housing demand. Population changes depend on birth, death, and migration rates. Household formation depends on marriage rates, the ability to live as a separate household (which is a function of income and the price of housing relative to the prices of other goods), preferences for separate living, and social attitudes toward the composition of the family. Many of these same factors affect the size of households. All other things equal, a decline in the average size of households would lead to an increase in the demand for dwelling units. As Table 1-1 indicates, average household size has fallen considerably during the last eighty years. In addition, the 1960 nonfarm population was roughly five times the 1890 nonfarm population. The decline in household size combined with population growth has led to an additional 52.6 million households—thus the demand for additional dwelling units between 1890 and 1970. Grebler, Blank, and Winnick have estimated that 80 percent of the new households formed between 1900 and 1950 was attributable to population growth, with the decline in average household size responsible for the remainder.[1]

The composition of the population (for example, age, household size and income) affect the distribution of housing demand among the different types of

Table 1-1

Nonfarm Population, Nonfarm Households and Average Nonfarm Household Size: 1890-1970

Year	Nonfarm Population (Millions)	Nonfarm Households (Millions)	Average Nonfarm Household Size
1890	33.500	7.923	4.23
1900	44.800	10.274	4.36
1910	59.895	14.132	4.24
1920	74.096	17.600	4.21
1930	92.618	23.300	3.98
1940	101.453	27.874	3.64
1950	127.649	37.089	3.44
1960	165.881	49.585	3.34
1970	192.624	60.516	3.18

Sources: Leo Grebler, David M. Blank, and Louis Winnick, *Capital Formation in Residential Real Estate* (Princeton: Princeton University Press, 1956), p. 82; U.S. Bureau of the Census, Census of Population: 1960, vol. 1, *Characteristics of the Population*. part 1. U.S. Summary (Washington, D.C.: U.S. Government Printing Office), Tables 65 and 185; U.S. Bureau of the Census, *Census of Population: 1970, General Social and Economic Characteristics, United States Summary*, Final Report PC(1)-C1 (Washington, D.C.: U.S. Government Printing Office, 1972), Table 85.

housing units. Consider the stages that a typical household would pass through in a lifetime: single and young; married, young and no children; married, middle-aged and young children; married, older and children grown; and widowed or retired. These stages in the family life cycle have often been used to categorize and predict household behavior. In the housing market, stages in the family life cycle lead to a residential cycle: (a) young single persons rent small apartments; (b) young married couples with no children rent larger apartments; (c) young married couples with young children buy a house; (d) married couples with school-age children buy a second larger house, usually in the suburbs, to be closer to better schools or because the family's income has increased; (e) married couples with children no longer at home may sell their house and either buy a smaller house or rent an apartment closer to the center of their metropolitan area; and (f) death of one mate may lead to living with relatives or renting an apartment.[2] This view of stages in the life cycle and the demand for housing suggests that renter households tend to be young, have few members (for example, very young children or none at all) and have small incomes. In fact, empirical studies indicate that these types of households have a higher probability of renting than do other types of households.[3] Data from the 1970 Census of Population and Housing confirm these earlier studies: 74.1 percent of the married male-headed households (wife present and no nonrelatives) with head under 25 years of age rent; 43.2 percent of those with heads 25 to 34 rent; 23.3

percent of those with heads 35 to 44 rent; 19.2 percent of those with heads 45 to 64 rent; and 21.6 percent of those with heads 65 years or older rent.[4] The slight rise in renting for older households and the high incidence of renting among young households are consistent with the residential cycle hypotheses. According to the 1970 census data, smaller households are more inclined to rent than larger ones: 57.3 percent of the one-person households rent. The percentage renting drops to 36 percent for two- and three-person households, 29.3 percent for four-person households, and 26.5 percent for five-person households. It climbs back to 29.6 percent for households with six or more persons, which is probably a reflection of a decline in per capita income as family size increases. The 1970 census data also shows that households with small incomes are the most likely to rent: approximately 50 percent of the households with incomes under $7,000 rent while only 15.5 percent of those with incomes of $25,000 or more rent. In between, 38.7 percent of those with incomes of $7,000 to $9,999 rent; 27.4 percent of those with incomes of $10,000 to $14,999 rent; and 19.6 percent of those with incomes of $15,000 to $24,999 rent.

The supply of housing adjusts to the demand for housing through alterations of the existing stock of dwelling units (conversions, mergers, demolitions, and variations in the level of services) and through new construction. Although both new construction and net conversions (conversions less mergers) have made major contributions to supplying this additional demand, their relative roles have varied substantially over the period. Between 1890 and 1930, new construction produced the bulk of the additions to the housing stock (Table 1-2). During the 1930s and 1940s, conversions played a much larger role in supplying additional housing units. New construction regained its dominant position in the 1950s. Replacement demand increased substantially during the 1950s, when nearly 2.7 million nonfarm dwelling units were demolished for road construction, urban renewal, and other activities, and were destroyed in disasters such as hurricanes and fires. This trend continued into the next decade; between 1960 and 1970, 6.59 million nonfarm dwelling units disappeared.[5] The 1960-70 figure combines conversions, mergers, demolitions, and disaster losses. However, it is so large and occurred during a period of active highway construction (the interstate system) and clearance for urban renewal, that it undoubtedly reflects a substantial increase in demolitions and disaster losses above the preceding decade. The multifamily housing stock suffered the largest losses: 16.9 percent compared with only 12.5 percent for the rest of the stock.[6] Most of these units were centrally located, and their loss probably increased the prices of centrally located units and thereby made suburban apartments relatively more attractive to apartment consumers. It should be noted that the estimates of conversions and demolitions are not highly reliable, and that the figures on housing starts are more reliable after 1940 than before. An additional source of nonfarm dwelling units is the movement of existing units from farm to nonfarm status.

Table 1-2

Changes in Number of Nonfarm Households and Dwelling Units, and Nonfarm Housing Starts, Conversions, and Demolitions: 1890-1970

Years	Increase in Nonfarm Households (Millions)	Increase in Nonfarm Housing Stock (Millions)	Nonfarm Dwelling Units Started (Millions)	Net Number of Dwelling Units Added by Conversion (Millions)	Dwelling Units Destroyed through Demolition or Disaster (Millions)
1890-1900	2.351	2.271	2.941	0.062	0.208
1900-1910	3.858	3.736	3.606	0.081	0.297
1910-1920	3.468	3.579	3.593	0.103	0.414
1920-1930	5.700	6.580	7.004	0.312[a]	0.590[a]
1930-1940	4.574	4.014	2.646	1.070	0.397
1940-1950	9.215	9.942	6.954	2.000	1.000
1950-1960	12.496	15.135	14.644	−0.008[b]	2.666[b]
1960-1970	10.931	10.771	13.878	NA	6.589[c]

[a]This figure is the average of the two estimates given by David L. Wickens and Lowell J. Chawner.

[b]Based on changes in the composition of the U.S. Housing Inventory 1950-1959.

[c]Includes conversions and mergers.

Sources: Grebler, Blank, and Winnick, *Capital Formation in Residential Real Estate*, pp. 86 and 329; U.S. Bureau of the Census, *Census of Housing: 1960*, vol. 4, *Components of Inventory Change*, Final Report HC(4), part 1, no. 1 (Washington, D.C.: Government Printing Office, 1962), Table C, p. 22; U.S. Bureau of the Census, *Census of Housing: 1970, Detailed Housing Characteristics, United States Summary*, Final Report HC(1)–B1 (Washington, D.C.: Government Printing Office, 1972), Table 21.

The Great Depression and Governmental Regulation

The high level of conversions during 1930-50 was a consequence of the Great Depression and governmental regulations that severely restricted residential construction during World War II. During the depression, many households ceased to exist as separate units because they could no longer afford the costs. This doubling up was undoubtedly responsible for the slowdown in the increase in nonfarm households during 1930-1940 (Table 1-2). In addition, many dwelling units were subdivided into several units; an increase in the number of dwelling units but a decrease in the housing services provided by one dwelling unit. The war controls encouraged similar behavior during 1941-1945. At the end of the war and with the depression over, these doubled up households and population growth resulted in an enormous demand for additional dwelling units.

During the depression and World War II—except for 1943—multifamily starts declined more precipitously than other starts. Governmental regulation during World War I appears to have had a similar effect (Figure 1-1). Perhaps part of the explanation is that multifamily housing units are on the average smaller than other units, and conversions may have been a relatively more effective supply mechanism for small units as opposed to large units. In fact, owner-occupied housing became less important during the depression, declining from 47.8 percent of the occupied stock in 1930 to 43.6 percent in 1940. Such a movement would be expected due to the generally larger size of owner-occupied units and their greater expense. In addition, new multifamily housing was probably not competitive with existing multifamily housing in the many large cities that extended rent control beyond World War II into the early 1950s.

The rise in multifamily starts in 1948-50 (Figure 1-1) was entirely the result of federal financial assistance under section 608 of the National Housing Act. Under this program the Federal Housing Administration (FHA) insured mortgages on multifamily housing carrying extremely liberal and attractive terms. In fact, many producers were able to "mortgage out"; that is, they were able to undertake and complete construction of section 608 developments with no investment of their own funds. As a result, it was a popular program with investors, many of whom were amateurs, until a congressional investigation into "windfall" profits dampened enthusiasm. Of the 532,000 project units (units in structures containing five or more units) started under FHA insurance between 1946 and 1952, over 80 percent (427,000 units) were insured under section 608.[7] The effect of this program on multifamily housing starts is illustrated by Figure 1-2. It is also clear from Figure 1-2 that FHA insuring policy has not been responsible for the recent growth in multifamily starts which preceded increases in FHA insured starts by several years. It is quite possible that much of FHA's activity in 1970 did not represent a net addition to the private housing inventory; that is, many of these FHA insured units might have been constructed in any case.

Underlying Patterns

When the depression and governmental regulation are accounted for, three phases are evident in Figure 1-1. During the first, which extends from 1900 to 1928, there is a slow but steady increase in the share of starts composed of multifamily units. Without World War I, there would not have been a decline in the late teens, and the 1928 peak might not have been as high. The second phase extends from 1928 to 1957. Although the depression was the cause of the sharp decline in 1929, the postdepression behavior in 1936-39 and 1945-57 indicates that multifamily starts' share of total starts would have begun to decline sometime in the early thirties had neither the depression nor World War II occurred. The third phase starts in 1957 and consists of a rapid increase in multifamily starts both absolutely and relative to total starts.

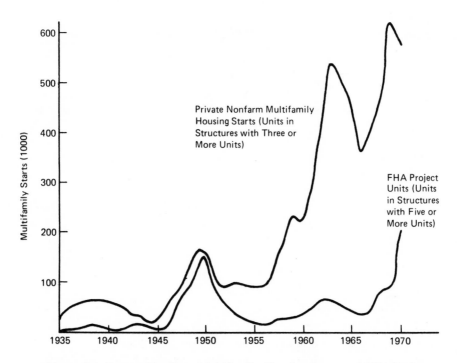

Figure 1-2. Private Nonfarm Multifamily Housing Starts and FHA Project Units: 1935-1970. Source: Appendix A.

These three phases can be understood in terms of the urbanization of the population, immigration, rising incomes, suburbanization, and the age distribution of the population. Since the founding of the United States, its population has become increasingly urbanized (Table 1-3). Nineteenth-century and early twentieth-century cities or urban areas tended to be monocentric in structure; that is, most of the employment opportunities and other activities were located at the center of the urban area. The cost (amount of time and out-of-pocket expenses) and means of transportation accounted for this concentration near waterways; railroad yards were also located centrally to tie up with water transport. Individual household members or workers were also constrained by transportation costs to live near their places of work and other activities; that is, in dense quarters (multifamily structures). These individuals had to rely on walking and the horse and buggy which were joined by streetcars in the late nineteenth century. The streetcars led to the construction of two- and three-family houses on 5000 square foot lots, still quite dense by the standards of today.[8] These forces are reflected in the decline in owner-occupancy during the 1890-1920 period (Table 1-3).

Innovations in production and transportation technology, starting in the early

8

Table 1-3
United States Population by Age, Urban Residence, Owner-Occupancy, and Car Registrations: 1850-1970

Year	Total Population (1000)	Population Aged 20-29 (1000)	Population Aged 20-29 as a Percent of Total Pop.	Percent Urban[a]	Percent of Occupied Dwelling Units Owner-Occupied	Car Registrations per Capita
1850	23,192	4,277	18.4	15.3	NA	–
1860	31,443	5,726	18.2	19.8	NA	–
1870	38,558	6,823	17.7	25.7	NA	–
1880	50,156	9,169	18.2	28.2	NA	–
1890	62,622	11,425	18.2	35.1	47.8	–
1900	75,995	13,864	18.3	39.7	46.1	0.0001
1910	91,972	17,237	18.7	45.7	45.8	0.0049
1920	105,711	18,363	17.4	51.2	45.6	0.0769
1930	122,775	20,703	16.9	56.2	47.8	0.1876
1940	131,669	21,685	17.2	56.5	43.6	0.2086
1950	150,697	23,724	15.7	59.0	55.0	0.2676
1960	179,323	21,670	12.1	–	61.9	0.3433
1970	203,212	29,848	14.7	–	62.9	0.4393

[a]The 1850-1950 data is calculated under the same definition of urban.

Source: U.S. Bureau of the Census, *Census of Population*; Hope T. Eldridge and Dorothy S. Thomas, *Population Redistribution and Economic Growth, United States, 1870-1950*, vol. 3, *Demographic Analysis and Interrelations* (Philadelphia, Pa.: The American Philosophical Society, 1964), pp. 196 and 198; U.S. Bureau of the Census, *Historical Statistics of the United States, Colonial Times to 1957; Continuation to 1962 and Revisions* (Washington, D.C.: U.S. Government Printing Office, 1965).

part of the twentieth century, have substantially altered the structure of the urban economy.[9] The development of assembly line and continuous processing techniques called for single-story plants requiring more land. The advent of the truck and automobile gave industries the locational freedom to select these sites away from the high-priced center of the monocentric cities. These changes are discussed in more detail in Chapter 2 in an examination of the location of multifamily housing within a metropolitan area. For present purposes, it is only necessary to realize that this suburbanization of industry greatly increased the worker's possibility for lower-density living. There is ample evidence of the preference to live at lower densities and to own one's home. When this greater mobility is coupled with rising real incomes brought about by World War II and sustained thereafter by the economy, it is no surprise that in the period 1936-57 the vast majority of starts were concentrated in structures containing less than three units. In fact, most of these starts were single-family houses; two unit structures fell from over 20 percent of starts in 1922-23 to only 2 percent in

1956. As a result, homeownership increased dramatically to 61.9 percent in 1960 (Table 1-3).

It is widely asserted that liberal Federal Housing Administration and Veteran's Administration mortgage terms for single-family, owner-occupied housing gave this submarket a substantial competitive advantage over rental housing. These programs, however, are more a reflection, through the political system, of the more basic changes in plant location and in household incomes. The major innovation of low down payment, long-term amortized mortgages was already underway in the 1920s; the contribution of FHA and VA was the earlier widespread acceptance of these ideas by the mortgage industry. Since these liberal lending terms are still available, they do not provide an explanation for the recent increase in multifamily starts.

Although rising real incomes in the period since World War II have increased the demand for owner-occupied (single-family) houses, a substantial change in the age composition of the adult population has played an important role in increasing the demand for multifamily housing since the mid-1950s. In Table 1-4, the age of the population is used as a proxy for the age of the head of the household. Up until 1930, the population between the ages of twenty and twenty-nine grew quite regularly and by sizeable amounts, except for the decade corresponding to World War I. This growth contributed to the demand for apartments in the monocentric cities of this period. Between 1930 and 1960, this segment of the population barely grew at all, a principal cause being the low birth rate during the depression which affected the 1950-60 period. Perhaps the

Table 1-4
Population Change by Age: 1850-1970

Years	Increase in Total Population (1000)	Increase in Population Ages 20-29 (1000)
1850-1860	8,251	1,449
1860-1870	7,115	1,097
1870-1880	11,598	2,346
1880-1890	12,466	2,256
1890-1900	13,373	2,439
1900-1910	15,977	3,373
1910-1920	13,739	1,126
1920-1930	17,064	2,340
1930-1940	8,894	982
1940-1950	19,028	2,039
1950-1960	18,626	−2,054
1960-1970	13,889	8,178

Source: U.S. Bureau of the Census, *Census of Population.*

decline in the 1930-40 period was attributable to the curtailment of immigration in the early 1920s. In the 1960s, there was a sharp increase in persons in this age group, a result of the World War II and postwar baby boom. The annual current population surveys conducted by the Bureau of the Census also provide information on the age distribution of the heads of households. This data, which is summarized in Table 1-5, suggests that the number of young households began to increase in the late 1950s. The number of households with heads under thirty years of age increased by a sizeable number in 1956. (The sample design for these surveys has changed over time, and an important change before the 1963 survey is probably responsible for the similarity between the 1962 and 1963 figures for households with heads under thirty.)

Changes in the cost of inputs to multifamily housing relative to other types of

Table 1-5
Number of Households by Age of Head: 1952-1971

Year	Number of Households	
	Total	Head Under 30 Years of Age
1952	45,464	6,404
1953	46,828	6,494
1954	46,893	6,147
1955	47,788	6,231
1956	48,785	6,592
1957	49,543	6,604
1958	50,402	6,672
1959	51,302	6,607
1960	52,610	6,852
1961	53,291	6,934
1962	54,652	7,243
1963	55,189	7,263
1964	55,996	7,636
1965	57,251	8,195
1966	58,092	8,516
1967	58,845	8,816
1968	60,446	9,133
1969	61,803	9,938
1970	62,874	10,406
1971	64,374	10,907

Source: U.S. Bureau of the Census, *Current Population Reports*, Series P-20, "Household and Family Characteristics" (Washington, D.C.: U.S. Government Printing Office, 1953-1972), Numbers 44, 53, 67, 75, 83, 88, 100, 106, 116, 125, 139, 153, 164, 173, 191, 200, 218, 233.

housing may be another factor contributing to the recent shift to multifamily housing. Unfortunately, the E.H. Boeckh indexes of the cost of constructing apartment buildings includes hotel and office buildings and does not reflect the construction costs of the garden-style apartments that have been so popular in the last twenty years. Therefore it is not possible to draw definitive conclusions about the influence of construction-cost differentials. The limited information contained in the Boeckh indexes of residential construction costs and apartment building costs (high-rise construction) indicates that apartments are becoming relatively more expensive to build.[10] Such a trend would favor residence construction and work against the simultaneous trend toward apartments. Therefore building-cost differentials do not appear to be responsible for the growth in multifamily starts.

The cost of land is another input to the development of housing accommodations. If the cost of land were rising, this would favor more intensive use of land such as the construction of apartments instead of single-family houses. It is widely asserted that land costs have been increasing very rapidly, and there is some supporting evidence.[11] This increase in the price of land (per square foot) can be viewed as the result of a decrease in the relative supply of land available for urban use given the stock constraint of existing uses.

In this century, the supply of land for urban use (commercial, industrial, and residential) has experienced substantial increases as a result of major transportation innovations. The car and truck greatly expanded the urban area that any firm or household could reasonably consider using for any given state of the rest of the world. The depression and World War II slowed down the response to these shifts in land supply, especially in those sectors in which the government did not have a wartime production interest such as commercial and residential. At the end of the war and throughout most of the fifties, the nation's urban housing markets adjusted to this change in the supply of land by expanding the urban area occupied by residential dwellings and building dwelling units at lower densities (primarily single-family homes in the suburbs). Since other factors— most importantly household income, easier credit terms, and plant technology— also changed in directions conducive to suburban low-density development, the response was broader than would have been experienced had there only been a change in the supply of urban land. In the last thirty years, however, there have been few changes in the transportation systems serving urban areas, and those that have occurred (expressways) have only been marginal and incremental. The airplane was the major innovation in transportation during this period, but it has had only minor effects on intrametropolitan mobility. Just as the earlier changes opened up more land to urban use, the use of that land during succeeding decades without major changes in transportation technology has reduced the supply of urban land available for new use (vacant land).

Since 1953 the Bureau of Labor Statistics has computed consumer price indexes for rental housing and for owner-occupied housing. According to these indexes, the costs of renting and owning followed almost identical price movements until 1965 when the cost of owning began to rise more rapidly than the cost of renting. In 1970 the rental index value (1957-59 equal 100) was 123.7 and the owning index value was 154.4. These imply that the consumer may find renting a better buy today than earlier. This differential, however, evolved long after the upswing in multifamily housing starts. In addition, these two consumer price indexes do not adequately reflect price movements because of the unusual difficulties associated with holding the bundle of housing attributes constant over time. Ownership also provides certain advantages over renting which these indexes do not take into account: lower cash outlay for the same quantity and quality of housing, and federal income tax benefits. A recent analysis of the costs of renting and owning suggests that home purchase pays if a household is likely to reside in it for three to five years.[12]

Summary

In a 1958 analysis of the rental housing market, Louis Winnick claimed that:

While moderate gains in apartment construction may be expected even if existing policies remain unchanged, a new and more positive rental-housing program is needed if the market potential of the future is to be fully realized.[13]

The preceding discussion shows that such a policy did not evolve but multifamily housing starts soared to their highest level in this century. In general this upswing and the other twentieth-century long swings in the share of starts that are in multifamily structures have been a function of changes in the urban economy, rising incomes, and the age distribution of the population. One implication is that as the young adults occupying the new multifamily housing units grow older, marry, and have children, single-family starts should increase their share. A decline in the birth rate during the late fifties and throughout the sixties implies a decline in young adults demanding apartments in the late 1970s and in the 1980s.

2 The Suburban Housing Market

Traditionally, housing has been discussed as if a dwelling unit were a homogeneous good, and up to this point I have treated housing as divisible into two homogeneous goods—multifamily and nonmultifamily units. The data available for analysis of national trends precludes a more detailed classification. It is well known, however, that housing is a very heterogeneous commodity. When a dwelling unit is purchased or rented, the consumer is really buying a bundle of services. Included in this bundle are (1) attributes of the structure and dwelling unit (floor area, room sizes, number of rooms, kitchen equipment, heating system, etc.); (2) neighborhood characteristics (density, characteristics of one's neighbors, architecture of other houses, etc.); (3) a bundle of public services (schools, highway maintenance, refuse collection and disposal, police and fire protection, etc.); (4) location (journey to work and other activities). In addition to this wide variation in the services associated with any given dwelling unit, the durability of housing constrains the amount of change which any given dwelling structure can be subjected to without demolition. All these factors make the housing market one of the most complex markets to study. In this study I will analyze new apartment construction in the suburbs and try to take explicit account of these factors.

Many of the multifamily units recently constructed have been built in the suburbs, even at the outer fringes of urban areas. Over the 1962-70 period, 52 percent of all multifamily starts (units in structures containing at least five units) in sixty-three large standard metropolitan statistical areas (SMSAs) have been located in their suburban rings (Table 2-1). In 1970 the mean number of multifamily starts in the ring was over 3,300 units for these same SMSAs. The figures in Table 2-2 illustrate the extent of multifamily housing development for some selected SMSAs over the 1962-70 period. In several cities the ring's share of multifamily starts exceeds 80 percent. Most of the SMSAs with low percentages (Houston, Tucson) are new growth areas with central cities containing a large share of the total SMSA population. Even some of the growth areas (Phoenix) are experiencing the suburbanization of apartment construction. This pattern is a break with the traditional location of multifamily housing and has important implications for urban form, transportation systems, and the provision of public services.

In order to understand the suburban multifamily housing market, recent trends in urban spatial structure and their motivating forces must be reviewed. Employment and population have been decentralizing throughout most of this

Table 2-1

Private Multifamily Housing Starts and Structure Size by Central City and Ring for Sixty-Three SMSAs: 1962-70

Year	Mean Percentage of SMSA Multifamily Starts in the Ring	Mean Number of Multifamily Units Started per Structure (Average Structure Size)		Mean Number of Multi-family Housing Starts in the Ring
		Central Cities	Rings	
1962	40.3	–	–	2,106
1963	44.4	–	–	2,723
1964	46.6	–	–	2,733
1965	51.0	–	–	2,694
1966	52.7	28	17	2,169
1967	56.5	31	17	2,652
1968	52.8	36	19	3,273
1969	57.3	33	19	3,493
1970	55.5	35	18	3,359
1962-1970	52.1	31	18	25,201

Source: U.S. Bureau of the Census, "Housing Units Authorized by Building Permits and Public Contracts," *Construction Reports*, Series C-40 (1962-1970). The sixty-three SMSAs are listed in Appendix B.

century. Robert Haig was perhaps the first scholar to take note of this trend in 1926.[1] The depression dampened the trend, and it did not resurface until World War II. The average annual value of construction put in place (constant 1957-59 dollars) fell from $9.8 billion during 1918-28 to $3.6 billion during 1928-38.[2] Although restrictions on materials' usage, construction, and investment were in force during the war years, they did not prevent the suburbanization of employment. The average outlays for industrial buildings rose from $1.1 billion during 1928-38 to $3.9 billion during 1938-46, a level higher than the averages for the 1946-53, 1953-57, and 1957-62 periods. (Most of this expansion consisted of public investment in industrial plants; after the war, nearly all of these facilities were transferred to private ownership, frequently at a nominal cost.) It appears very likely that much of this construction occurred at the periphery of central cities, often within their legal boundaries. Population movement was, however, effectively slowed by wartime controls. Although the average outlays for residential construction increased from $3.6 billion during 1928-38 to $5.3 billion during 1938-46, they were still below the predepression level and only 36 percent of the 1946-53 figure.

In the postwar periods, both population and employment suburbanized (used interchangeably with decentralization) at a rapid pace. Between 1948 and 1963, suburban rings (the area inside a standard metropolitan statistical area but

Table 2-2
Percentage of Private Multifamily Housing Starts Located in the Ring for Selected SMSAs: 1962-70

SMSA	Percentage
Baltimore	67.0
Boston	59.9
Buffalo	80.0
Chicago	62.4
Cleveland	83.8
Dallas	30.9
Denver	43.9
Detroit	84.7
Fresno	29.1
Houston	13.5
Jersey City	78.3
Memphis	29.2
Miami	81.3
Newark	88.3
Oklahoma City	29.8
Omaha	18.9
Peoria	28.5
Philadelphia	77.2
Phoenix	39.8
Pittsburgh	67.9
Rochester	78.7
Sacramento	70.8
St. Louis	78.2
San Antonio	9.3
San Francisco-Oakland	69.5
San Jose	66.3
Tucson	17.1
Washington, D.C.	81.3

Source: See Table 2-1.

outside its central city) grew faster than the central cities, and suburban employment grew at a faster rate than suburban population. The average annual percentage change in central city employment and population never exceeded 3.9 percent and had many declines. In every employment category (manufacturing, wholesaling, retailing, and services) and all three time periods (1948-54, 1954-58 and 1958-63), the annual percentage changes for central cities were substantially smaller than those for the suburban rings. According to John Kain:

Except for manufacturing during 1954-1958 and 1958-1963, the average yearly percentage increases in [suburban] employment exceeded 10 per cent for all four employment categories and three time periods. . . . Yearly percentage increases in suburban population, though considerable, are only about half as large as the increases in suburban employment.[3]

Examination of the mean absolute changes in employment and population for the central cities and suburban rings also support these observations. In Table 2-3, these same categories along with multifamily housing (units in buildings with at least three units) are examined for the 1963-67 period. These figures have been corrected for annexation following the procedure used by Kain.[4] Again, the suburban rings have higher rates of growth than the central cities. The mean annual percentage increase in manufacturing employment is 7.2 percent in the ring and 2.3 percent in the central city. For wholesaling, the figures are 15.4 percent in the ring and 2.0 percent in the central city; for retailing, 7.8 percent in the ring and 1.9 percent in the central city; and for services, 12.3 percent in

Table 2-3

Estimated Mean Annual Percentage and Absolute Changes[a] in Population, Employment, and Multifamily Housing for Central Cities and Rings of Sixty-one Large SMSAs (1960 Central City Boundaries)

Item	Percentage			Absolute		
	SMSA	Central City	Ring	SMSA	Central City	Ring
Employment (1963-67)						
Manufacturing	3.8	2.3	7.2	4677	1089	3588
Wholesaling	5.1	2.0	15.4	1413	353	1060
Retailing	4.3	1.9	7.8	2565	507	2057
Services	6.3	4.2	12.3	1916	1020	896
Population (1960-70)	2.2	0.8	3.5	23682	2371	21491
Multifamily Housing (1960-70)	7.9	3.4	42.6	4569	1425	3144

[a]Simple, unweighted averages of individual area percentage and absolute changes.

Sources: Calculated from published data obtained from the following publications: U.S. Department of Commerce, Bureau of the Census, *Census of Manufactures: 1963, vol. 3, Area Statistics*; *Census of Manufactures: 1967, vol. 3, Area Statistics*; *Census of Business: 1963, vol. 2, Retail Trade-Area Statistics*; *Census of Business: 1963, vol. 5, Wholesale Trade-Area Statistics*; *Census of Business: 1963, vol. 7, Selected Services-Area Statistics*; *Census of Business: 1967, vol. 2, Retail Trade-Area Statistics*; *Census of Business: 1967, vol. 4, Wholesale Trade-Area Statistics*; *Census of Business, vol. 5, Selected Services-Area Statistics*; *Census of Population: 1970, General Population Characteristics*; *Census of Housing: 1960, Metropolitan Housing Characteristics*; *Census of Housing: 1970, Detailed Housing Characteristics*. The sixty-four SMSAs are listed in Appendix C. (Jacksonville and Nashville-Davidson are excluded because their metropolitan-wide forms of government eliminate the ring; Albany-Schenectady-Troy is excluded because some information on the central cities was suppressed.)

the ring and 4.2 percent in the central city. Ring population has grown at a rate over four times as fast as central city population, and ring multifamily housing has grown at a rate over ten times that in the central cities. The high mean annual percentage increase in ring multifamily housing is in part due to a small base. However, the figures on mean absolute changes show suburban rings with larger increases than the central cities in all categories except services.

The more rapid growth of employment in the suburbs relative to population suggests that the redistribution of employment is a crucial determinant of metropolitan form and structure. If employment is divided into population-serving and nonpopulation serving employment, it is reasonable to expect movements in the first category to be proportional to population changes and movements in the second category to be relatively independent of the distribution of population within the metropolitan area. Several factors are responsible for the redistribution of employment. In general, a firm (old, new, or expanding) would seek a location that maximizes its profits, which reduces to cost minimization when revenues do not vary spatially and to revenue maximization when costs are spatially invariant. Although one of the factors determining profitability is access to a suitable work force, two major technological innovations have minimized the importance of this factor on the location decisions of firms within any given metropolitan area. In the area of production technology, new methods (assembly line, continuous processing, and new materials-handling techniques such as the forklift truck) require horizontal plants, usually single-story, which demand larger tracts of land than prior techniques. Land was available in the suburbs and outlying parts of central cities at lower prices than near the center (no demolition costs, no holdout costs, and a declining rent surface with distance from the central business district). The other innovation has been in the area of transportation. The truck has freed the plant from dependency on waterways and railroad lines to receive inputs and to ship its product. The car has greatly increased the worker's mobility and hence reduced the firm's concern with access to the work force, especially with plenty of suburban land for parking lots. As a result, cost differentials for labor, rent, property taxes, and material inputs between central city and suburban plant locations should favor the suburbs. A recent study of these cost differentials for manufacturing firms in the Boston metropolitan area found that "these differentials are sufficient to cut the absolute level of net operating profits in the central city by 15 to 30 percent over those prevalent at suburban sites."[5] This study concludes that

further net losses of central city [manufacturing] employment are contained only by the fact that many central city firms have sunk costs associated with earlier decisions to locate there and that other firms, specialized manufacturing plants, operate according to production considerations different from those taken as "average."[6]

Firms producing unstandardized products, small firms whose size makes them dependent on other entities for services, and firms employing a large proportion of low-wage, low-skill workers fall in this latter category.

A Model of Residential Location Decisions

The preceding discussion of urban development implies that household location decisions are made with reference to their workplaces. A rough schematic of this process is shown in Figure 2-1. The arrows are intended to describe the dominant direction of relationships that have some simultaneity. Theories of residential location have concentrated on working households; the location decisions of the unemployed and retired have not received much attention.

The simplest theories of residential location assume a uniform featureless plain (transportation equally possible in all directions and no legal, social, or other restrictions on transactions in the urban land market) and all employment to be located at the center (Alonso, Mills, Muth, and Wingo).[7] Households are assumed to maximize utility subject to a budget constraint. The analysis focuses on the consumption of residential space, transportation (mainly the journey to work), all other goods lumped together, and income. The journey to work is singled out because it is the dominant trip and is one of the few trips with both

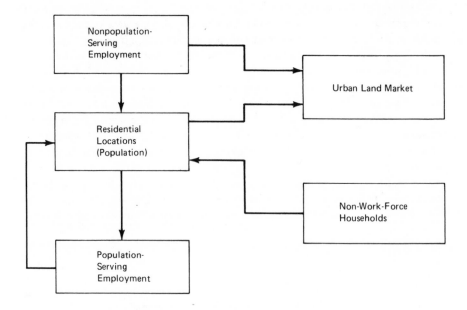

Figure 2-1. Urban Development Process.

frequency and regularity as to destination. It is also assumed that residential space is not an inferior good and that travel (commuting) is an inferior good. The models state that households trade the costs of housing consumption against the costs of making a longer journey to work. That is, for a given workplace and bundle of housing attributes (most of the monocentric theories treat housing as a homogeneous good), households try to minimize their total location costs and not simply the monetary and time costs of the work trip. For example, a household that wants a relatively large bundle of housing attributes will generate net savings by incurring increased work trip costs, because that large bundle is cheaper away from the center. Differences in the price of any given bundle are due principally to spatial variations in land values, which are highest at the center. In general these monocentric theories imply that population density will decline with distance from the center; Muth and Mills have made various further assumptions that allow them to characterize this decline as an exponential decay. These monocentric theories also suggest that rising real incomes and a positive space preference lead to lower density residential development. Up to 1958, most suburban residential development consisted of low-density, single-family dwelling units in response to rising real incomes after World War II. The long run equilibrium nature of these theories ignores the durability of the housing stock, and the monocentric assumption contradicts the substantial suburbanization of job locations.

The pattern of apartment construction in the 1960s points up the inadequacy of these simple theories of urban form. The monocentric theories suggest that as a metropolitan area's population increases (all other things constant), the area occupied by higher density housing should expand somewhat in the manner depicted in Figure 2-2. The changes between 1960 and 1970 in the geographical distribution of apartments along two sectors of the Boston metropolitan area are illustrated in Figures 2-3 and 2-4. Both demonstrate the inappropriateness of the monocentric theories of residential location. Multiple peaks were present in 1960 and became accentuated in the following decade. The pattern of changes in the percentage of the housing stock in structures containing two or more units along either corridor cannot be explained without reference to multiple workplaces. At a minimum one would expect each workplace to act similarly to a miniversion of the monocentric models of urban form. Since land prices would tend to be higher near employment centers, population density would increase and, in particular, multifamily housing would be expected to develop around these centers. In Figures 2-3 and 2-4, the peaks occurring at roughly a distance of ten miles from Boston's central business district along both corridors correspond to the intersections between Route 128, a major circumferential limited-access highway and suburban employment center, and the major radial highways in each sector. In a recent study of San Francisco, Mahlon Straszheim found that rents increase in the immediate vicinity of suburban job concentrations.[8]

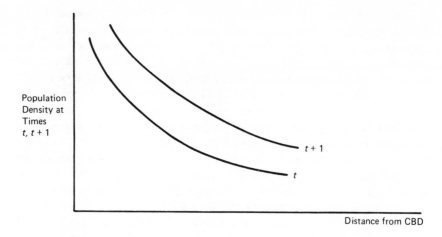

Figure 2-2. Monocentric View of Suburbanization of Apartments.

The multiple workplace case can be examined by considering the residential location decision of a household relative to its workplace.[9] It is necessary to assume that the rent gradient declines in at least one direction from the workplace. The following assumptions are also made: a household's transportation cost function increases with distance from its workplace(s); households maximize utility; there is a market for residential space; the workplace is known, and residential space is not an inferior good. Marginal cost curves for the journey to work (including the value of travel time) and for housing services are shown in Figure 2-5. If this household desires to consume q_2 units of housing service, its optimal residential location is at i where its total location costs are a minimum. Multiple workplaces act as a decentralizing force; this can be seen by starting with a monocentric world and letting one household have a decentralized workplace. A household with a noncentral workplace but also desiring to consume q_2 units of housing service would select a location farther from the center than a similar household who worked in the center. This is illustrated in Figure 2-6. With multiple workplaces, the rent surface along one corridor might have several peaks as in Figure 2-7. One of the major objectives of this study is to examine the demand for suburban apartments as a function of the changing geographic distribution of employment. Theories of residential location imply that the suburbanization of employment should be accompanied by suburban apartments. This is one of the hypotheses to be tested in the next two chapters.

The timing of the aforementioned technological innovations has had important implications for urban form. Urban areas that had not grown significantly prior to these innovations developed in a low-density pattern. Older cities, which had substantial durable stocks of housing and other structures as well as street

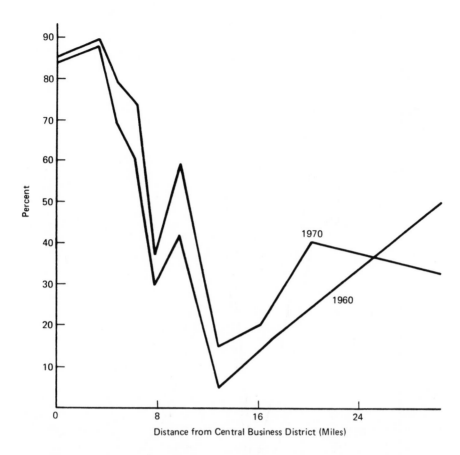

Figure 2-3. Percentage of all Housing Units which are in Structures with Two or More Units by Distance from the Boston Central Business District for Cities and Towns on or adjacent to the Massachusetts Turnpike: 1960 and 1970.

patterns suited to an older technology, were hampered in their ability to respond freely to these new techniques. For example, the city of Los Angeles is an urban area which developed after the major innovations in transportation and plant technology. As a result, it has many relatively well-defined dispersed subcenters, each of which has a healthy apartment market. In older cities, which contained large stocks of multifamily housing, the development of a suburban multifamily housing market may have been retarded due to an excess supply of such housing in the central city. Any analyses comparing different SMSAs must control for these differences in urban form.

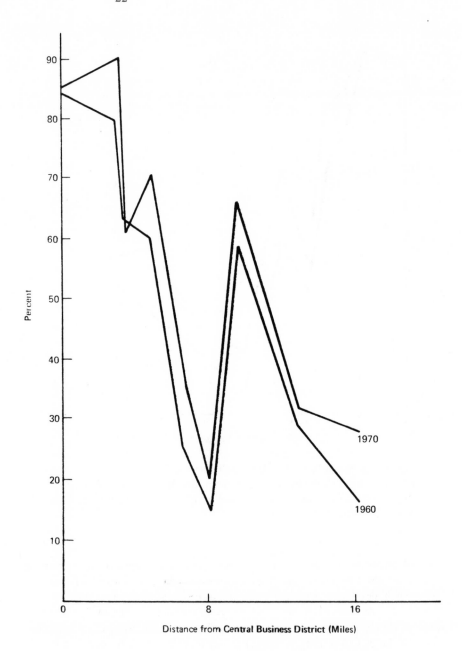

Figure 2-4. Percentage of all Housing Units which are in Structures with Two or More Units by Distance from the Boston Central Business District for Cities and Towns on or adjacent to I-95: 1960 and 1970.

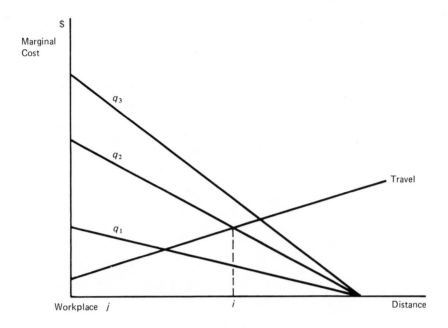

Figure 2-5. Marginal Cost Curves.

Implications for Housing Markets

The possibility of an excess supply of multifamily housing in the 1946-55 period must be examined more closely. During World War II, rising real incomes increased demand for more spacious housing (including lot size). In addition, transportation innovations increased the feasible commuting distance by lowering the marginal cost of transportation, which reduced the price of residential land by increasing its supply. As a result, the demand for single-family houses on their own lots increased because they had become relatively less expensive. Governmental restrictions on residential construction during World War II prevented the satisfaction of this demand. Although the value of private starts in the 1938-46 period was higher than the figure for 1928-38 and the value of public starts increased tenfold, together they were barely half the predepression level and not even a third of the 1946-53 level.[10] During the war period, households were compelled to live in housing substantially removed from their equilibrium situation, multifamily units, when they preferred lower density structures. When the controls were removed, the market began to adjust to this unsatisfied demand. Figure 2-8 depicts demand and supply in the large-lot submarket over time. It assumes that the market was in long-run equilibrium in 1940. The shift in demand is due to rising real income; the demand is greater in

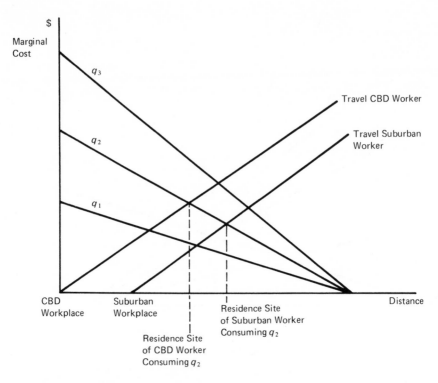

Figure 2-6. Marginal Cost Curves and Suburbanization of Employment.

the suburbs because of the suburbanization of employment and decreased commuting costs. Only slight expansion of the supply was permitted until 1946. As a result, the prices in the central city large-lot submarket ($P^L_{CC,46}$) and the suburban large-lot submarket ($P^L_{SS,46}$) were in disequilibrium and greater than their equilibrium prices, P^{EL}_{CC} and P^{EL}_{SS}, respectively. After the controls were removed, the supply of large-lot housing expanded to bring the market back into equilibrium. (The discussion is framed in equilibrium terms only for purposes of simplifying the exposition.)

The shift in demand to the large-lot submarket was accompanied by a decrease in demand in the small-lot submarket (Figure 2-9). Rent control and restrictions on residential construction maintained occupancy and the profitability of these units. The small-lot submarket was forced to absorb the unsatisfied demand for large-lot housing until the governmental controls were removed. When the controls were removed, vacancies increased in the small-lot (multifamily) submarket. The supply, however, did not decrease because of the durability of the stock. Consequently, rents in the small-lot submarket declined.

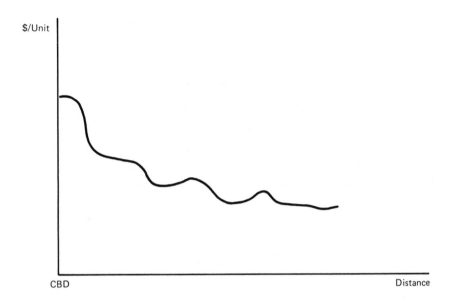

Figure 2-7. Rent Surface with Multiple Workplaces.

In general, evidence bearing on these changes is difficult to obtain. However, the monthly rent (deflated by the consumer price index) of apartments built before 1940 and located within metropolitan areas is available for four points in time. (Nearly all of these units were located at the center of the various metropolitan areas.) The monthly rent on these units dropped from $64 in 1940 to $55 in 1950, and increased to $78 in 1960 and $84 in 1970.[11] The rent decline observed for 1950 is consistent with the present discussion. New construction would not be expected in this submarket without governmental assistance. In fact, almost all of the multifamily housing built between 1946 and 1952 was financed under the very liberal terms of the federal government's section 608 program. In the central city, demand for small-lot housing probably continued to decline after the war. In the suburbs, demand for small-lot housing probably suffered smaller declines and eventually increased. Therefore the 1955 position of the demand curve in the suburbs is not sketched in Figure 2-9. The main implication is that the rent surface in the multifamily housing market was very likely inverted at the close of World War II. That is, centrally located multifamily units were less expensive than peripherally located units of equal quality.

What does this rent inversion look like when the rent must decrease at the urban fringe (agricultural land)? The rent surface must be peaked. From Figure 2-10, it is possible to see that a household preferring to live in an apartment and with its head working at j would select a central city apartment. This choice will

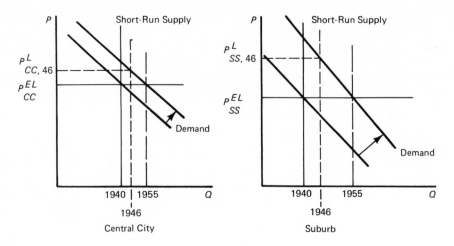

Figure 2-8. Large-lot Submarket.

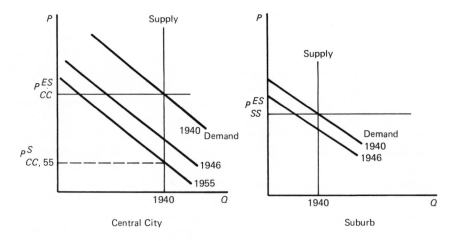

Figure 2-9. Small-lot Submarket.

minimize the household's total location costs (housing costs plus work-trip costs). Consequently, apartment dwellers would be expected to be reverse commuters in the early 1950s. $T(j)$ represents total commuting costs from j. RR is drawn to represent the rent necessary to attract private capital to this submarket for the construction of new units. Since RR lies above the rent surface at all points, there is insufficient demand to attract private funds for new units.

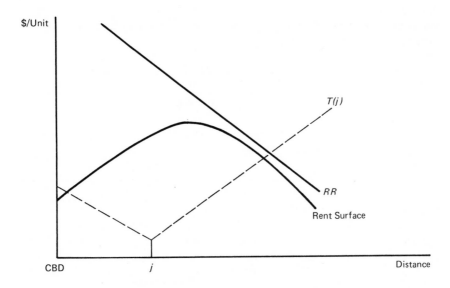

Figure 2-10. Rent Inversion in the Small-lot Submarket.

In fact, Chicago (1956) and Detroit (1952) whites working in the suburbs and residing in apartments were often reverse commuters in the 1950s.[12] The data in Table 2-4 further illustrates the extent of reverse commuting among suburban-employed apartment dwellers. The Detroit metropolitan area has been divided into six rings centered on the central business district. Each ring is progressively further from the center of the metropolitan area; ring 1 is the central business district and contains very little housing. Nearly two-thirds of the workers employed in ring 4 and choosing to occupy apartments (buildings with three or more units) resided in residence zones closer to the center than their workplace. Over 70 percent of ring 5 workers choosing apartments lived closer to the center than their workplace. The effect declines for ring 6 workers, but even then nearly 30 percent of those choosing apartments live in rings 2 and 3, the two closest residential rings.

The situation pictured in Figure 2-10 has changed with time. Many multi-family housing units have been constructed with private capital since 1957, and many of these units have been built in suburban locations. Several forces are responsible for this change. Part of the explanation lies in the demographic changes discussed in Chapter 1; in summary, the number of households who traditionally have been apartment dwellers has been on the increase throughout this period. Changes in the structure of the local housing market are equally, perhaps more, significant. In Figure 2-10, the multifamily housing stock, aside

Table 2-4

Percentage of Outer Employment Ring Workers Residing in Each Ring, by Structure Type: Detroit, 1952

Structure Type	Residence Ring						
	1	2	3	4	5	6	Total
	Percentage of Ring 4 Workers						
One-family	–	2.6%	13.4%	34.2%	30.7%	19.1%	100%
Two-family	–	8.2	39.4	42.8	7.1	2.5	100
Multiple	–	21.5	43.2	25.5	5.1	4.7	100
All	0.5%	6.0	21.4	34.5	23.3	14.4	100
	Percentage of Ring 5 Workers						
One-family	–	0.7%	6.0%	16.3%	51.8%	25.1%	100%
Two-family	–	5.2	27.0	31.8	30.2	5.9	100
Multiple	–	12.9	34.4	24.2	17.9	10.5	100
All	0.3%	2.2	10.5	18.4	46.8	21.8	100
	Percentage of Ring 6 Workers						
One-family	–	0.8%	3.4%	7.3%	24.0%	64.5%	100%
Two-family	–	3.2	21.2	25.7	10.2	39.8	100
Multiple	–	9.8	18.2	10.3	9.5	52.2	100
All	0.4%	2.0	6.2	9.2	21.2	61.0	100

Source: John F. Kain, "The Journey to Work as a Determinant of Residential Location," *Papers and Proceedings of the Regional Science Association* 9 (1962): 156. (Table XI). Reprinted with permission of the Regional Science Association.

from its locus, is viewed as a homogeneous good, all units being of equal quality. As the decade of the 1950s progressed, the quality and volume of the central city's multifamily housing stock depreciated due to (1) decreased maintenance necessary to rent at below equilibrium prices, (2) demolitions for highways and urban renewal, (3) declines in the level of public services, and (4) declining neighborhood quality (including elements of discrimination in the choice of neighbors). Furthermore, the costs of rehabilitating the low quality existing stock exceeded the rents that could be demanded given the level of neighborhood quality and public services in the central city. (This same process is probably part of the cause of abandonment in central-city, low-income areas; even the lowest income groups want more than those neighborhoods now provide.) This process is illustrated in Figure 2-11 by viewing the central-city multifamily housing market as composed of two quality submarkets (poor and good). Figure 2-11 illustrates the resultant shift of units from the good quality submarket to the poor quality submarket. A major consequence of this shift was an increase in the price of good quality central city housing (from P_1 to P_2),

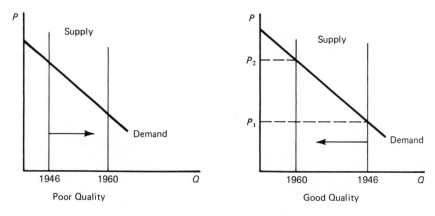

Figure 2-11. Central City Multifamily Housing Market.

which removed the rent inversion. There was no longer an excess supply of good quality multifamily housing in the central city. The existence of a rent inversion in the apartment submarket in the 1950s implies that even after its removal in the 1960s, the rent surface in this submarket would be less steep than the rent surface in the large-lot submarket. Straszheim finds just such a relationship for San Francisco in 1965. He reports that

housing prices for a house standardized for quality (5.5 rooms, built since 1960, and on a lot ranging in size from 0.2 to 0.3 acre) ranges from $57,000 in several zones near the center of San Francisco to $20,000 in distant suburbs (a 50-minute commute). Rent variation for a standardized apartment (a 4-room apartment, built since 1960) is much less, from $185 to $110. The rent gradient is less steep than the owner-occupied housing gradient.[13]

Straszheim's results, however, are also consistent with other explanations. For example, given the larger role of land as an input to single-family housing relative to multifamily housing, it would be reasonable to expect that the ratio of the price of single-family housing units to the price of multifamily housing units would be higher in central areas than in outlying areas. In other words, the multifamily housing rent gradient would be flatter than the single-family housing rent gradient—precisely Straszheim's result.

An additional explanation of the shift of apartment development to the suburbs is that since 1950 the suburban prices of single-family housing have increased relative to the suburban prices of multifamily housing units with rising land costs playing a major role. As suburban single-family housing became more expensive relative to suburban apartments, the demand for apartments in the suburbs increased. Although such changes played an important part in the development of a suburban apartment market, they do not explain the rather large degree of reverse commuting by suburban workers to central city apartments in the 1950s. The concept of a rent inversion during this period does explain this phenomenon. Of course, it would be desirable to compare the degree of reverse commuting in the 1950s with the degree of reverse commuting after the construction of a large number of suburban apartments during the 1960s.

When the rent inversion disappeared, households that had been commuting from suburban workplaces to central city apartments began to demand suburban apartments, and their offer price increased above the rents necessary to attract private capital to the suburban multifamily housing market. The force underlying these changes in the local housing market is the suburbanization of industry, delayed by the excess supply of good quality central city apartments at the end of World War II. In addition, many of the new households demanding apartments (the demographic changes discussed in Chapter 1) are either the offspring of suburban families or suburban households about to retire. As such, they have roots in suburbia and an attachment to various lifestyles. The young households cannot afford single-family housing and are probably at a point in their life cycle where they prefer apartments, while the older households may want less responsibility. Both groups, however, wish to remain in the suburbs and enter the suburban multifamily housing market. Since there was relatively little existing multifamily stock in suburban areas, the demand has been reflected directly in new construction.

3

The Demand for Multifamily Housing in Metropolitan Areas

The process of urban development is one of stock adjustment. Changes in demand for various structure types and hence net residential density are reflected in the incremental additions to, and subtractions from, the housing stock. Twentieth-century American urban areas have experienced a long-run decrease in net residential density. A recent study by David Harrison and John Kain shows that the percentage of new construction which consists of single-family dwelling units (a proxy for net residential density) increased by more than 8 percent each decade over 1870-1960.[1] In addition, Edwin Mills has calculated density gradients for the period 1880-1963 for each of four metropolitan areas.[2] His results also show a long-term trend toward lower density residential areas which was in progress as early as 1880. Both studies show more rapid rates of low-density development in the 1910-19 and 1945-54 periods which correspond closely with the introduction of the automobile and the relaxation of wartime controls. It is interesting that for the most recent period in Mills' analysis (1958-63), the rate of suburbanization was the slowest, below the average for the entire period (1880-1963) and less than half the highest rate, which occurred during 1948-54. Harrison and Kain's analysis also indicates a slight slowdown in the trend at the end of their period; they attribute this to observed values of the dependent variable close to its maximum value.

Commuting costs and family income are important determinants of the density of development, and the density of past and future development depends on the values of these variables at the time of development (see Chapter 2). However, reliance on these factors alone to explain changes in net residential density assumes that other characteristics of the population remain static over time. In fact, there have been substantial changes in the age distribution of the population during the last twenty years (see Chapter 1). One consequence has been an increase in multifamily housing, which probably explains the decline in the rate of low-density development detected by Mills, Harrison, and Kain. In order to examine the effect of the boom in multifamily housing construction on the patterns of urban development, the Harrison-Kain model is used to simulate the two most recent periods: 1960-64 and 1965-70. Their model relates the percentage of new construction, which consists of single-family dwelling units (S^*), to metropolitan area size (dwelling units in thousands at the beginning of the time period (H)) and time (T). There are thirteen time periods which constitute the time variable.[3] They estimate two functional forms of the model: one uses the number of dwelling units and the other uses the logarithm of the number of dwelling units. Their estimates are:

$$S^* = 17.06 + 8.34T - 0.015H$$
$$(16.3) \quad (47.4) \quad (-12.1) \qquad\qquad 3.1$$

$$R^2 = 0.68$$

$$S^* = 25.66 + 10.58T - 5.99 \log H$$
$$(23.8) \quad (46.4) \quad (-17.3) \qquad\qquad 3.2$$

$$R^2 = 0.71$$

These equations are used to predict S^* for 1960-64 and 1965-70 for each of sixteen standard metropolitan statistical areas (SMSAs). These predicted values are compared to the actual values in Table 3-1. It is evident that this model does not perform well in the most recent decade; the predicted values are 20 to 30 percentage points above the actual values. The Harrison-Kain model predicts substantially more low-density development than has occurred. In order to investigate the detailed nature of the time trend, they reestimate Equations 3.1 and 3.2 with dummy variables for each time period in place of T. This version shows the accelerating effect of the automobile in 1910-19, the deceleration due to World War II restrictions, and the flattening of the time trend in the late 1950s. It is now clear that this flattening is, in large part, due to the increase in multifamily housing construction, which began in 1958. If this version were reestimated, including the two most recent periods, there would probably be a decided deceleration in the time trend toward lower density urban development. Although this discussion has relied on a comparison of the actual and predicted values of S^* in sixteen SMSAs, only 67.9 percent of new construction during 1960-64 was single-family; the figure for 1965-70 was even lower, 58.6 (Table 3-1). It appears that this phenomenon is widespread.

Since much of the multifamily housing that has been constructed since 1958 is not as dense as that built during the early twentieth century, the result of today's market response to the large increase in young households has been a lower density suburban apartment environment than at an earlier point in time. That is, within the apartment submarket, a time trend toward lower density apartments can be observed. These new apartments, however, are built at a higher density than the increment in urban development added during 1920-58. At the same time, the aging of this cohort will probably produce a return to the basic trend of low-density development; the late 1970s and the 1980s will see an increase in the construction of single-family housing.

Demand Functions

Household preferences for single-family, two-family, or multifamily housing are generally viewed as dependent on family size, age, income, and education.

Table 3-1

Percentage of New Construction which is Single Family—Actual and Predicted Values for 1960-64 and 1965-70 and Selected SMSAs

SMSA	S* for 1960-64			S* for 1965-70		
	Actual	Predicted		Actual	Predicted	
		H-K1	H-K2		H-K1	H-K2
Atlanta	67.9	92.6	93.2	55.4	96.8	96.8
Baltimore	69.0	89.1	89.2	54.8	93.3	93.8
Boston	64.0	85.2	86.6	43.9	89.4	91.5
Chicago	59.8	70.4	81.5	49.9	74.6	86.1
Dallas	70.1	91.8	92.0	56.4	96.0	95.7
Denver	69.3	92.4	92.9	61.2	96.6	96.8
Detroit	80.6	81.0	84.7	62.8	85.2	89.4
Los Angeles- Long Beach	43.7	68.7	81.1	41.6	72.9	85.4
Louisville	82.4	93.5	94.8	64.6	97.7	99.2
Oklahoma City	87.3	94.2	96.7	73.5	98.4	100.5
Phoenix	75.1	93.9	95.7	73.0	98.1	98.9
Pittsburgh	84.5	86.6	87.4	66.6	90.8	92.2
Portland	73.3	92.6	93.2	60.7	96.8	97.6
Richmond	71.4	94.5	97.5	62.4	98.7	101.7
San Jose	62.1	93.7	95.3	63.6	97.9	98.3
Syracuse	71.5	94.0	96.1	54.5	98.2	100.8
All SMSAs	67.9	–	–	58.6	–	–

Source: The actual values were computed from "Year Structure Built" by "Units in Structure" tables in U.S. Bureau of the Census, *Census of Housing: 1970. Metropolitan Housing Characteristics* (Washington, D.C.: Government Printing Office, 1972), Table A-6 (one for each SMSA). The predicted values were obtained from the Harrison-Kain equations. H-K1 refers to Equation 3.1, and H-K2 refers to Equation 3.2: see the text.

Recent evidence also suggests that the job locations of working members of the household also affect household decisions about structure type. James Brown and John Kain have investigated the probability of a household choosing a particular housing type using data from the San Francisco Bay Area Transportation Study Commission's origin and destination survey.[4] A binary variable represents the choice of a particular housing type; it has a value of one for the house type in question and zero otherwise. This variable is regressed against dummy variables representing the socioeconomic characteristics and workplace of the household.[5]

Several different sets of submarket definitions were investigated, but the one comparing apartments to all other structure types bears on the present discussion. The coefficients for the apartment equation estimated with ordinary least squares indicate that the probability of households with heads under thirty years of age choosing apartments (units in buildings with at least three units) is 4 percent greater than the probability of households with heads over sixty. In contrast, households with heads between thirty and sixty years of age are 8 percent less likely to choose an apartment than the oldest households and 12 percent less likely to choose apartments than the youngest households. Households with three or four members are shown to be 24 percent less likely to choose an apartment than households with one or two members; larger households are even less likely to choose an apartment. Households with a college-educated head are 4 percent more likely to choose an apartment than other households. Families with income between $4,000 and $10,000 are 10 percent less likely to choose an apartment than those with incomes less than $4,000; families with higher incomes are even less likely. The Bay Area is also divided into six workplace zones; five are represented by dummy variables and the sixth, which is composed of outlying areas surrounding the cluster of five, is represented in the intercept. The results indicate that households with heads working in San Francisco are 14 percent more likely to choose an apartment than those with heads employed in the outlying areas. Households with workers in Oakland, the Peninsula (both sides of the bay), and San Jose are 11 percent more likely than those with workers in the outlying areas to choose apartments. If the head's workplace is in the valley (Marin County north of San Francisco and the area east of the bay centered on Walnut Creek), the household is 4 to 7 percent less likely to choose an apartment than if the head worked in San Francisco, Oakland, the Peninsula, or San Jose, but still 7 percent more likely to choose an apartment than if the head worked in the outlying areas. In summary, suburban work locations tend to reduce the probability of choosing an apartment because of smaller differences between the prices of suburban apartments and suburban single-family houses.

One important question is still unanswered: if the households were choosing to live in suburbia for reasons independent of structure type, how would their workplace affect their probability of choosing an apartment. The Brown-Kain study does not address this issue, but Franklin James and James Hughes have in a recent study of New Jersey.[6] They use data from the home interview survey conducted by the Tri-State Regional Planning Commission, and pattern their analysis after Brown and Kain's work. Their results for household income, family size, age of head, and workplace are virtually identical to those of Brown and Kain. (James and Hughes did not have an education of head variable.) In addition, James and Hughes repeat the above analysis while restricting the sample to households working in the New York-New Jersey metropolitan region but residing in New Jersey. Although their earlier analysis of all households shows that households working in Manhattan tend to be least likely to choose single-family homes and most likely to choose apartments, their analysis of households residing in New Jersey shows that those households working in Manhattan and living in New Jersey are . . . more likely to choose single-family homes than are households employed in five of the nine Northeastern New Jersey counties included in the Tri-State region. It seems clear that the households commuting from New York are commuting to New Jersey *in order to obtain* single-family homes.[7]

People's attitudes and behavior change as they pass through the stages of life. In the present context, young single persons are probably more likely to select multifamily housing than a married couple in their 40s with two young children. The age of head and household size variables that have been employed in earlier studies are an attempt to capture changes in behavior accompanying movement through the family life cycle. It would be more direct and informative to define the relevant stages in the family life cycle and use them as independent variables. For example, one study using life-cycle stages detected that widows and widowers tend to give up homeownership, a result obscured by the presence of older married couples over sixty-five in studies comparing rates of homeowner-ship with the age of head.[8] Structure choice functions, similar to Brown and Kain's, are estimated for a 1960 sample of the households residing in metropolitan areas with one-half million or more persons using stages in the family life cycle as independent variables in place of age and size.[9] An assumption implicit in this analysis is that the markets under investigation were close to equilibrium in April 1960 when the data was gathered. Since multifamily housing starts turned upward scarcely three years earlier and in view of the possibility of a rent inversion in the multifamily housing market, it is quite possible that the multifamily housing market was not in equilibrium in 1960. As a result, the probabilities of selecting an apartment, especially a suburban one, are likely to be underestimated. Although such disequilibrium makes interpretation of the quantitative results more difficult, analysis of the data is still fruitful.

The dependent variable is again dichotomous (a value of one representing an apartment and a value of zero all other structure types) and is interpreted as the conditional probability of a household selecting an apartment. (Since the dependent variable is dichotomous, the R-square statistic does not provide much useful information.) The independent variables are all dummy variables. Households are stratified into fifteen life-cycle categories or stages. There are three age groups (under thirty years of age, thirty to sixty years old, and sixty or more years old). Each age group is subdivided. The youngest group is divided into single, married with no children, married with children, and others (divorced, separated, and widowed). The middle-aged group is subdivided into single, married with no children, married with children under six, married with children at least six years old, widows and widowers, and divorced or separated persons. The oldest age group is divided into the same categories except married households with children are not differentiated by the age of the children. A household's stage in the family life cycle is represented by assigning that stage a value of one and all other stages a value of zero. All but one of the fifteen stages is represented in this way by a dummy variable in the regression. Income is divided into four categories: under $4,000, $4,000 to $9,999, $10,000 to $14,999, and $15,000 or more. The income category representing each household's income is assigned a value of one, and all other categories of income a value of zero. Education is divided into two categories: more than high school education and high school or less. Workplace is represented by dummy variables for the central city and suburban ring. Households with heads working outside the SMSA are grouped with nonworkers because of insufficient observations and are reflected in the intercept. The intercept also reflects the structure choice probabilities of divorced, separated, or widowed households under thirty years of age with income under $4,000 and less than college education.

The probability of a household choosing multifamily housing depends on the price of multifamily dwelling units relative to the price of other structure types such as single-family dwelling units as well as on the household's stage in the life cycle, its education (a taste variable), its income, and its workplace. The ratio of these prices is likely to vary from one metropolitan area to another. Since the 1960 sample used here is drawn from SMSAs all across the country, heed must be given to variations in this ratio. Since the land costs are higher in larger metropolitan areas, multifamily housing is probably less expensive relative to other structure types (e.g., single-family units) in these larger metropolitan areas than in the smaller ones. For this reason, two sets of equations are estimated: one set for SMSAs with one million or more persons in 1960 and one for those with more than one-half but less than one million persons.

The present study is particularly interested in the choice of an apartment in the suburbs which involves a decision to choose an apartment over other structure types and a decision to choose the suburbs over the central city. James and Hughes examine the first given that households had selected the suburbs; they do not investigate the choice between the suburbs and the central city. A parallel analysis with the 1960 sample produces results similar to theirs; that is, given that a household chooses the suburbs, the probability of living in an apartment is greater if the head works in the suburban ring. Such an approach, however, ignores an important part of the process: the selection of a residential area. The present study examines the reduced form as a joint choice by estimating the probability of living in a *suburban apartment*.[10] It also examines the probability functions for central city apartments, other structures (nonmultifamily housing) in the suburbs, and apartments in general. The parameters in all equations are estimated with ordinary least squares.[11]

The results for the largest metropolitan areas are summarized in Table 3-2. The best way to visualize the results for the stages in the life cycle is to construct what might be called the conventional progression of stages: young and single, married with no children, married with young children, married with older

Table 3-2

Probability of Choosing Various Structure Types for Households Residing in SMSAs Containing One Million or More Persons: 1960[a]

	Multi-family Housing Units	Suburban Multi-family Housing Units	Central City Multi-family Housing Units	Suburban Housing Units in Other Structure Types
Single, under 30	0.1605	0.0358	0.1248	−0.0302
	(3.79)	(1.64)	(3.15)	(−0.69)
Single, 30-60	0.0909	0.0080	0.0829	0.0080
	(2.41)	(0.41)	(2.36)	(0.21)
Single, 60 or over	0.0638	0.0076	0.0562	0.0368
	(1.52)	(0.35)	(1.43)	(0.85)
Married, No Children, under 30	−0.0632	0.0339	−0.0971	0.1136
	(−1.57)	(1.64)	(−2.58)	(2.75)
Married, No Children, 30-60	−0.2038	−0.0454	−0.1584	0.1824
	(−5.81)	(−2.51)	(−4.83)	(5.05)
Married, with Children, under 30	−0.2226	−0.0392	−0.1835	0.2448
	(−6.14)	(−2.10)	(−5.42)	(6.57)
Married, Youngest Child under 6, 30-60	−0.2987	−0.0689	−0.2297	0.3035
	(−8.51)	(−3.81)	(−7.01)	(8.41)
Married, youngest Child 6 or Older, 30-60	−0.3220	−0.0774	−0.2447	0.3028
	(−9.18)	(−4.28)	(−7.46)	(8.39)
Married, with Children, 60 or over	−0.3197	−0.0589	−0.2608	0.2324
	(−6.75)	(−2.42)	(−5.90)	(4.78)
Married, No Children at Home, 60 or over	−0.2519	−0.0553	−0.1966	0.2049
	(−7.15)	(−3.05)	(−5.98)	(5.66)
Widowhood, 60 or over	−0.1835	−0.0220	−0.1614	0.1633
	(−5.10)	(−1.19)	(−4.80)	(4.41)
Widowhood, 30-60	−0.1517	−0.0380	−0.1137	0.1219
	(−4.02)	(−1.96)	(−3.22)	(3.14)
Divorced or Separated, 30-60	−0.0277	−0.0102	−0.0175	0.0474
	(−0.75)	(−.54)	(−0.51)	(1.25)
Divorced or Separated, 60 or over	−0.0171	−0.0428	0.0257	0.0336
	(−0.36)	(−1.77)	(0.59)	(0.69)
Income $4,000 to $9,999	−0.1000	0.0075	−0.1074	0.0734
	(−10.8)	(1.57)	(−12.4)	(7.71)
Income $10,000 to $14,999	−0.1534	−0.0033	−0.1502	0.1212
	(−11.9)	(−0.49)	(−12.5)	(9.13)
Income $15,000 or more	−0.1862	−0.0059	−0.1803	0.1930
	(−11.3)	(−0.70)	(−11.8)	(11.4)
More than High School Education	0.0199	0.0259	−0.0060	0.0522
	(2.32)	(5.87)	(−0.75)	(5.92)
Workplace in the Central City	0.0644	−0.0276	0.0920	−0.1704
	(6.95)	(−5.79)	(10.6)	(−17.9)

Table 3-2 (cont.)

	Multi-family Housing Units	Suburban Multi-family Housing Units	Central City Multi-family Housing Units	Suburban Housing Units in Other Structure Types
Workplace in the Suburban Ring	−0.1167 (−11.1)	0.0416 (7.71)	−0.1583 (−16.2)	0.3129 (29.1)
Intercept	0.5751 (16.99)	0.0891 (5.11)	0.4860 (15.4)	0.1343 (3.86)
R^2 (Corrected)	0.14	0.03	0.15	0.24
F	126.9	27.4	136.8	234.9
N	15,121	15,121	15,121	15,121

[a]t-statistics in parentheses.

children, married with children departed from the home, and widowed. It is expected that the probability of selecting an apartment is highest for the young and single group and that it decreases until the children have left home. In Figure 3-1, the probability of choosing a multifamily housing unit regardless of location within the metropolitan area is plotted against the progression of stages in the conventional life cycle, and the variation in structure choice over the life cycle is confirmed. Single persons under thirty years of age are 48 percent more likely to select an apartment than thirty-to-sixty-year-old, married households, whose youngest children are at least six years old. Although widows and widowers over sixty years old are 34 percent less likely than single persons under thirty to select an apartment, they are 14 percent more likely than the thirty-to-sixty-year-old, married households with older children (six or more years old) to select an apartment. The behavior of households headed by divorced or separated persons does not vary with age at the two-tailed 5 percent significance level; they are 16 percent less likley than young singles and 32 percent more likely than thirty-to-sixty-year-old, married households with older children to select an apartment. Figure 3-1 is drawn for a household with $10,000 to $14,999 income, less than high school education, and a workplace in the central city. Varying any one or a combination of these factors just shifts the curve up or down without affecting the differential probability between any two stages in the family life cycle. As household annual income increases, the household becomes less likely to select an apartment. Households with annual incomes in the $4,000 to $9,999 range are 10 percent less likely to select an apartment than are households with incomes less than $4,000 and 9 percent more likely to select an apartment than households with incomes over $15,000. Education has only a weak effect; households with college-educated heads are only 2 percent more likely to choose an apartment than households headed by

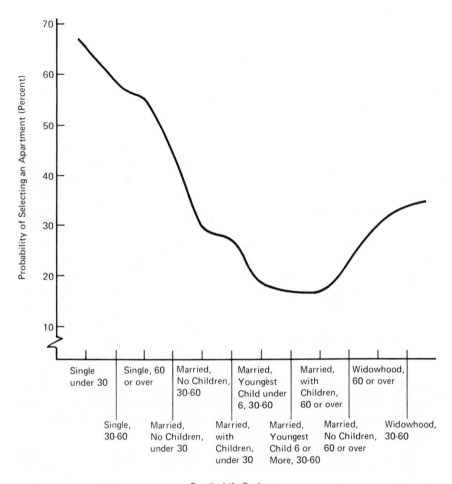

Figure 3-1. Probability of Selecting an Apartment by Family Life Cycle for Families with $10,000 to $14,999 Income, Less than College Education and Working in the Central City: Metropolitan Areas with One or More Million Persons in 1960.

persons with less education. Households with heads working in the central city are 6 percent more likely to select an apartment than households with no workers and those with workers employed outside the SMSA. The central city workers were 18 percent more likely than suburban workers to live in an apartment.

The equations for joint choice of structure and residential area also exhibit strong family life-cycle variations. The probability of selecting a suburban apartment is highest for the young and single, lowest for households with children at home, and in between for widowed households (Table 3-2). However, single households over thirty years of age are less likely than married households under thirty with no children to select a suburban apartment. The t-statistics reported in Table 3-2 test the hypothesis that the coefficients are significantly different from zero; that is, they are testing whether households in each of the stages in the family life cycle included in the regression are statistically different than divorced or separated households under thirty years of age—the intercept or reference point. The more interesting comparisons are often between stages in the life cycle included in the regression; statistical tests on these comparisons involve the standard errors of both coefficients, and two coefficients that are not statistically different than zero but have opposite signs could be statistically different from one another. This is probably the case for widowhood versus single under thirty. The variation in the probability of selecting a central city apartment with stages in the family life cycle is identical to that for the probability of choosing an apartment any place within the SMSA. As would be expected, the variation in the probability of selecting a nonmultifamily housing unit in the suburbs with stages in the family life cycle is the reverse of the pattern for multifamily housing; that is, families with children are most likely to select single-family and two-family housing units in the suburbs, and young singles are least likely.

College education contributes positvely to the selection of both types of suburban structures, but is negatively and insignificantly related to the choice of a central city apartment. One possible implication of these results is that college education has more to do with selecting a residential area than with selecting a structure type.

The probability of selecting a suburban apartment changes very little with income, while households with income over $15,000 are 19 percent more likely than those with incomes under $4,000 to select a single-family or two-family house in the suburbs. At the same time, high income households are 18 percent less likely than low-income households to select a central city apartment. The invariance of the probability of selecting a suburban apartment as income changes may be due, in part, to the disequilibrium of the suburban apartment market in 1960, which may also explain the low level of the probability of selecting a suburban apartment relative to the number of suburban apartments that have been constructed in the last decade. The high sensitivity of central city apartments and suburban nonmultifamily housing units to income changes in opposing directions suggests moves from central city apartments to suburban single-family housing as income increases. The workplace coefficients suggest that such moves are likely to be made by households with the head employed in the central city. The probability of consuming a central city apartment is 25 percent higher for central city workers than for suburban workers. Suburban workers are 48 percent more likely than central city workers to select a single-family or two-family house in the suburbs, and 7 percent more likely than central city workers to select a suburban apartment. The income elasticity (negative) of central city apartment demand is sufficient to counteract the negative effect of central city workplace on the selection of a suburban single- or two-family house. For example, a married couple with children, under thirty years of age, with more than $15,000 income and working in the central city would, in probabilistic terms, select a single- or two-family house in the suburbs over a central city apartment, whereas the same family with only $4,000 to $9,999 income would select the central city apartment.

Separate estimates of the income, education, and work-place coefficients were made for each of fourteen stages in the family life cycle to examine variations in tastes.[12] The results for multifamily housing any place in the metropolitan area are reported in Table 3-3. An analysis of covariance revealed statistically significant differences in preferences for structure types by stage in the life cycle. When the fourteen equations in Table 3-3 are tested against one equation including only income, education, and workplace variables, the F-statistic is 15.63.[13] Although the F-statistic for the comparison of the fourteen separate equations with the single-equation model including dummy variables for each stage in the life cycle (Table 3-2) is only 3.83, both statistics are significant at the two-tail one percent level. These two tests indicate that much of the variation across stages in the life cycle is in the constant term. At the same time, the coefficients of workplace, education, and income vary by stage in the life cycle. Although households with a suburban workplace are always less likely to select an apartment, the coefficients of the two workplace variables exhibit an interesting and consistent pattern of variation by stage in the life cycle. In general, place of work has the smallest effect for households with children present. The difference between the two workplace coefficients is smallest for married, thirty-to-sixty-year-old households with children over six (12 percentage points) and for married, thirty-to-sixty-year-old households with at least one child under six (13.5 percentage points); this difference is highest for never married (single) persons sixty or more years of age (34 percentage points), widowed households sixty or more years of age (33 percentage points), and divorced or separated households under thirty and sixty or more years of age (36 percentage points). The differential for married households with no children, young singles, and middle-aged widows lies between these extremes. The presence of children in a household not only substantially reduces the probability of selecting an apartment (Table 3-2) but also reduces the differential impact of workplace. Although workplace still has a statistically significant effect (at the two-tailed 5 percent level) on the probability of households with children selecting a multifamily housing unit, a change in workplace from the suburbs to the central city does not have a large effect on this probability.

Education is a statistically significant variable (two-tailed 5 percent level) for

Table 3-3
Probability of Selecting Multifamily Housing Stratified by Stages in the Family Life Cycle for Metropolitan Areas of One Million or More Persons: 1960[a]

	Income $4,000 to $9,999	Income $10,000 to $14,999	Income $15,000 or more	More than High School Education	Workplace in the Central City	Workplace in the Suburban Ring	Intercept	R^2 (Corrected)	F	N
Single, under 30	-0.0487 (-0.84)	-0.7922 (-3.05)	0.2427 (0.55)	0.0439 (0.79)	0.0788 (1.21)	-0.1786 (-2.17)	0.7134 (12.4)	0.06	3.72	268
Single, 30-60	-0.0241 (-0.58)	-0.1989 (-2.49)	-0.1506 (-1.26)	0.1340 (3.25)	0.0562 (1.20)	-0.2522 (-4.33)	0.6228 (14.9)	0.08	9.60	635
Single, 60 or over	-0.1569 (-2.26)	-0.0777 (-0.56)	-0.3844 (-1.73)	-0.0160 (-0.22)	0.1985 (2.72)	-0.1442 (-1.34)	0.6320 (16.1)	0.04	2.74	278
Married, No Children, under 30	-0.0362 (-0.58)	-0.0683 (-0.74)	0.1017 (0.50)	0.1296 (2.47)	-0.0677 (-0.97)	-0.3077 (-4.04)	0.5452 (7.79)	0.07	5.92	378
Married, No Children 30-60	-0.1191 (-4.51)	-0.1672 (-5.31)	-0.2493 (-6.38)	0.0861 (3.75)	0.0251 (1.03)	-0.1776 (-6.69)	0.4153 (15.0)	0.06	27.1	2386
Married, with Children, under 30	-0.2109 (-6.55)	-0.3335 (-4.98)	-0.3362 (-2.43)	0.0114 (0.39)	0.0456 (1.13)	-0.1409 (-3.32)	0.4640 (11.4)	0.08	16.7	1118
Married, Youngest Child under 6, 30-60	-0.2409 (-10.1)	-0.3201 (-10.9)	-0.2885 (-7.89)	-0.0219 (-1.60)	0.0348 (1.56)	-0.1002 (-4.25)	0.4275 (15.9)	0.08	36.9	2600
Married, Youngest Child 6 or over, 30-60	-0.1101 (-4.25)	-0.1474 (-5.25)	-0.1936 (-6.07)	-0.0419 (-2.72)	0.0159 (0.80)	-0.1089 (-5.22)	0.2965 (10.5)	0.05	24.8	2796
Married, with Children, 60 or over	-0.0755 (-0.91)	-0.2248 (-2.22)	-0.2660 (-2.32)	0.1113 (1.16)	0.0085 (0.13)	-0.1603 (-1.90)	0.2861 (3.91)	0.04	2.05	162
Married, No Children, 60 or over	-0.0550 (-2.23)	-0.0439 (-1.20)	-0.1435 (-3.31)	0.0249 (0.82)	0.1054 (4.18)	-0.0904 (-2.88)	0.2705 (15.3)	0.02	7.93	1727

Widowhood, 60 or over	-0.1096 (-3.08)	-0.2100 (-2.63)	-0.0028 (-0.03)	-0.0777 (-1.40)	0.2209 (5.00)	-0.1097 (-1.68)	0.3774 (20.9)	0.03	6.94	1087
Widowhood, 30-60	-0.1162 (-2.76)	-0.2014 (-2.15)	0.0490 (0.36)	0.1038 (1.80)	0.0899 (2.05)	-0.1975 (-3.31)	0.4161 (11.9)	0.05	6.38	594
Divorced or separated, 30-60	-0.0092 (-0.23)	-0.0265 (-0.30)	-0.2259 (-1.83)	0.0922 (1.94)	0.0242 (0.58)	-0.2108 (-3.90)	0.5298 (16.2)	0.03	5.29	767
Divorced or separated, under 30 and 60 or over	0.0051 (0.08)	0.1573 (0.78)	0.2915 (0.59)	0.0261 (0.32)	0.1758 (2.72)	-0.1856 (-1.93)	0.5066 (13.6)	0.03	2.79	318

[a]t-statistics in parentheses.

only four stages in the life cycle: single, thirty to sixty years of age; married, no children, under thirty years of age; married, no children, thirty to sixty years of age; married, youngest child six or over, thirty to sixty years of age. Households with college education in the first three of these stages (single or no children) have a higher probability of selecting an apartment than similarly situated households having less than college education. The difference in probability varies from 9 to 13 percentage points. The fourth stage in the life cycle for which education is statistically significant (married with older children) indicates that having a college education will reduce the probability of selecting an apartment by a small amount (4 percentage points). Education is not a particularly strong variable, and it is difficult to ascribe meaning to the statistically significant effects exhibited for some life cycles.

As a household's income increases, it would be expected to become more inclined to purchase a single-family house, and its probability of choosing an apartment would decline. Since parents in general believe that children in the home require both more interior and exterior space, income increases should have the largest reduction in the probability of selecting an apartment for households with children. According to the estimates in Table 3-3, households with children have the highest income coefficients and show the clearest pattern of declining probability of selecting an apartment as income increases. Middle-aged, married couples with no children also fall into this group. All but one of the fifteen income coefficients for these stages in the life cycle are statistically significant at the two-tailed 5 percent level. Divorced and separated households under thirty and sixty or more years of age exhibit the opposite pattern; their probability of selecting an apartment increases with income although none of the coefficients are statistically significant. The income coefficients for the remaining stages do not follow a consistent pattern. The most interesting of these are the young married households with no children and the young singles which show an increase in the probability of selecting an apartment for the highest income category, although statistically insignificant at the two-tailed 5 percent level. One explanation of this for the young married might be the two-worker household. If both spouses were at work, then their household income would be high but neither spouse would spend enough time at home to cause them to consider a single-family house. To examine this explanation, the households in this stage of the family life cycle are divided into two groups: those with more than one member in the labor force and those with less than two members in the labor force. The two-worker household hypothesis is disproved in separate estimates of the model for each group which show the probability of selecting an apartment to be higher for households with income of $15,000 or more than for households with income less than $4,000, regardless of the number of members in the labor force.

The results for suburban multifamily housing are presented in Table 3-4. As above, the stratification by family life cycle is statistically significant at the two-tailed one percent level. (F = 5.83 for the comparison to one equation including only income, education, and workplace, and F = 3.83 for the comparison to one equation which also included dummy variables representing fourteen stages in the family life cycle.) Households in every stage in the family life cycle are more likely to select an apartment if they work in the suburban ring. The differential effect of working in the central city versus the suburban ring is largest for never married (single) households, widowed, divorced, and separated households varying from 10 to 34 percentage points depending on age. For all other households the difference is small, ranging from one percentage point for elerly couples with children to 7 percentage points for young married couples with and without children. College education has a positive effect on the probability of selecting a suburban apartment whenever it is statistically significant (married, no children, under thirty years of age; married, no children, sixty or more years of age). In general, the income variables do not seem to be very important. When their coefficients are statistically significant, their behavior resembles that found for multifamily housing throughout the metropolitan area.

Residents of smaller metropolitan areas (population between one-half and one million) exhibit a similar pattern of behavior (Table 3-5). The only differences are: (1) the education variable has virtually no effect on the probability of structure choice (very small, statistically insignificant coefficients); (2) the decline in the probability of choosing an apartment, a suburban apartment, or a central city apartment as income increases breaks down for the highest income category; (3) the increase in the probability of selecting a suburban single- or two-family house as income increases also breaks down for the highest income category; (4) divorced and separated households are less likely to select apartments, particularly suburban apartments; (5) the stages in the family life cycle do not perform as well in the equation for single- and two-family houses in the suburbs; (6) both central city and suburban workers are less likely to choose an apartment than households with no workers or non-SMSA workers. However, suburban workers have a higher probability of choosing a suburban apartment than do central city workers. There are insufficient observations to conduct an analysis of covariance by stages in the family life cycle for these smaller metropolitan areas; only six of the fifteen stages could be separately estimated.

In summary, young, childless, highly educated, lower income households are more likely than other households to choose apartments. Consequently, the increase in young households in the 1950s and 1960s led to a large increase in the demand for apartments. If the head is employed in the more developed parts of a metropolitan area, these households are even more likely to choose apartments, which may be in part a reflection of the constraint placed upon choices by the historical pattern of urban development. At the same time, the dispersal of employment opportunities from the central part of metropolitan

Table 3-4

Probability of Selecting Suburban Multifamily Housing Stratified by Stages in the Family Life Cycle for Metropolitan Areas of One Million or More Persons: 1960[a]

	Income $4,000 to $9,999	Income $10,000 to $14,999	Income $15,000 or more	More than High School Education	Workplace in the Central City	Workplace in the Suburban Ring	Intercept	R^2 (Corrected)	F	N
Single, under 30	-0.0143 (-0.34)	-0.0457 (-0.24)	-0.1494 (-0.46)	0.0177 (0.44)	-0.0860 (-1.81)	0.2259 (3.74)	0.1317 (3.13)	0.10	6.03	268
Single, 30-60	0.0826 (3.22)	-0.0589 (-1.20)	0.1932 (2.63)	0.0323 (1.28)	-0.0858 (-2.99)	0.1321 (3.70)	0.0670 (2.62)	0.10	13.4	635
Single, 60 or over	0.0138 (0.33)	-0.0280 (-0.33)	-0.0433 (-0.32)	-0.0011 (-0.03)	-0.0538 (-1.21)	0.2897 (4.42)	0.0867 (3.64)	0.07	4.23	278
Married, No Children, under 30	0.0216 (0.49)	-0.0028 (-0.04)	0.0292 (0.21)	0.1265 (3.43)	-0.1150 (-2.33)	-0.0475 (-0.89)	0.1509 (3.07)	0.04	3.41	378
Married, No Children, 30-60	-0.0063 (-0.48)	-0.0069 (-0.44)	-0.0257 (-1.31)	0.0442 (3.84)	-0.0208 (-1.71)	0.0369 (2.77)	0.0481 (3.46)	0.02	7.61	2368
Married, with Children, under 30	-0.0272 (-1.51)	-0.0489 (-1.31)	0.0047 (0.06)	0.0357 (2.19)	-0.0342 (-1.52)	0.0358 (1.51)	0.0803 (3.52)	0.02	4.43	1118
Married, Youngest Child under 6, 30-60	-0.0147 (-1.30)	-0.0290 (-2.07)	-0.0273 (-1.57)	0.0011 (0.15)	-0.0289 (-2.71)	0.0115 (1.03)	0.0587 (4.58)	0.01	6.18	2600
Married, Youngest Child 6 or over, 30-60	-0.0029 (-0.26)	-0.0015 (-0.12)	-0.0268 (-1.94)	0.0107 (1.61)	-0.0229 (-2.66)	-0.0013 (-0.14)	0.0362 (2.95)	0.01	4.07	2796
Married, with Children, 60 or over	-0.0908 (-2.30)	-0.1113 (-2.31)	-0.1088 (-1.99)	-0.0097 (-0.21)	-0.0067 (-0.22)	0.0092 (0.23)	0.1156 (3.31)	0.01	1.37	162
Married, No Children, 60 or over	0.0237 (2.18)	0.0112 (0.70)	0.0170 (0.89)	0.0387 (2.87)	-0.0259 (-2.34)	0.0316 (2.29)	0.0225 (2.89)	0.01	5.06	1727

Widowhood, 60 or over	-0.0268 (-1.42)	-0.0698 (-1.65)	0.0140 (0.30)	-0.0018 (-0.06)	-0.0229 (-0.98)	0.1490 (4.29)	0.0723 (7.53)	0.02	4.31	1087
Widowhood, 30-60	-0.0297 (-1.55)	-0.0613 (-1.43)	0.0799 (1.29)	0.0003 (0.01)	-0.0341 (-1.71)	0.0580 (2.13)	0.0700 (4.39)	0.02	3.45	594
Divorced or Separated, 30-60	0.0405 (1.94)	0.0122 (0.26)	0.0305 (0.47)	0.0455 (1.82)	-0.0490 (-2.31)	0.1615 (5.66)	0.0498 (2.88)	0.09	13.3	774
Divorced or Separated, under 30 and 60 or over	0.0721 (2.11)	0.1024 (1.01)	0.0133 (0.05)	-0.0250 (-0.61)	-0.0293 (0.91)	0.1938 (4.04)	0.0411 (2.20)	0.07	5.17	318

[a] t-statistics in parentheses.

Table 3-5

Probability of Choosing Various Structure Types for Households Residing in SMSAs Containing One-half to One Million Persons: 1960[a]

	Multi-family Housing Units	Suburban Multi-family Housing Units	Central City Multi-family Housing Units	Suburban Housing Units in Other Structure Types
Single, under 30	0.1532 (2.06)	−0.0409 (−1.04)	0.1941 (2.91)	−0.1555 (−1.63)
Single, 30-60	0.0021 (0.03)	−0.0998 (−2.93)	0.1019 (1.77)	−0.0540 (−0.66)
Single, 60 or over	−0.0083 (−0.12)	−0.0961 (−2.58)	0.0878 (1.40)	−0.0850 (−0.95)
Married, no children, under 30	−0.793 (−1.21)	−0.1189 (−3.42)	0.0396 (0.67)	−0.0323 (−0.39)
Married, no children, 30-60	−0.2395 (−4.05)	−0.1124 (−3.58)	−0.1270 (−2.39)	0.0566 (0.75)
Married, with children, under 30	−0.2190 (−3.66)	−0.0992 (−3.12)	−0.1199 (−2.23)	0.0598 (0.78)
Married, youngest child under 6, 30-60	−0.2990 (−5.08)	−0.1272 (−4.06)	−0.1717 (−3.25)	0.1224 (1.62)
Married, youngest child 6 or over, 30-60	−0.3071 (−5.21)	−0.1209 (−3.86)	−0.1862 (−3.52)	0.1032 (1.36)
Married, with children, 60 or over	−0.3243 (−4.56)	−0.1516 (−4.00)	−0.1727 (−2.70)	−0.0062 (−0.07)
Married, no children, 60 or over	−0.3116 (−5.26)	−0.1241 (−3.94)	−0.1875 (−3.52)	0.0586 (0.77)
Widowhood, 60 or over	−0.2362 (−3.92)	−0.1131 (−3.53)	−0.1231 (−2.27)	0.0068 (0.09)
Widowhood, 30-60	−0.1873 (−2.97)	−0.1011 (−3.01)	−0.0862 (−1.52)	−0.0169 (−0.21)
Divorced or separated, 30-60	−0.1261 (−2.05)	−0.0834 (−2.55)	−0.0427 (−0.77)	−0.0354 (−0.45)
Divorced or separated, 60 or over	−0.0840 (−1.15)	−0.0993 (−2.57)	0.0153 (0.23)	−0.0728 (−0.78)
Income $4,000 to $9,999	−0.0687 (−5.27)	−0.0095 (−1.37)	−0.0592 (−5.05)	0.0686 (4.10)
Income $10,000 to $14,999	−0.1276 (−6.13)	−0.0283 (−2.55)	−0.0993 (−5.31)	0.1403 (5.25)
Income $15,000 or more	−0.0941 (−3.31)	−0.0175 (−1.16)	−0.0766 (−3.00)	0.1383 (3.79)
More than High School Education	−0.0093 (−0.69)	0.0008 (0.11)	−0.0100 (−0.83)	0.0316 (1.84)
Workplace in the Central City	−0.0191 (−1.37)	−0.0407 (−5.52)	0.0217 (1.74)	−0.1434 (−8.05)
Workplace in the Suburban Ring	−0.0519 (−3.23)	0.0180 (2.11)	−0.0699 (−4.84)	0.2992 (14.5)

Table 3-5 (cont.)

	Multi-family Housing Units	Suburban Multi-family Housing Units	Central City Multi-family Housing Units	Suburban Housing Units in Other Structure Types
Intercept	0.4755 (8.29)	0.1736 (5.69)	0.3018 (5.85)	0.2936 (3.99)
R^2 (Corrected)	0.10	0.03	0.10	0.16
F	25.8	7.28	25.4	44.8
N	4,579	4,579	4,579	4,579

[a]t-statistics in parentheses.

areas to the suburbs has led to increased apartment construction in the suburbs because suburban workers are more likely to select a suburban apartment than are central city workers.

Stock Adjustment Model

These probability models can be used in conjunction with a stock adjustment model to examine changes in the composition of the housing stock over time, assuming that the price of apartments relative to the price of single-family houses does not change. Stock adjustment models have been used to study the investment decisions of business organizations and to estimate the price and income elasticities of the demand for housing.[14] According to this model, a change in the housing stock over a period of time is proportional to the excess of the number of housing units demanded at the end of a time interval (the desired stock) over the actual number in supply at the beginning of the interval (actual stock). In addition, there is some replacement demand, which is normally assumed proportional to the actual stock. That is,

$$\Delta H = \alpha(H_t^d - H_{t-1}) + \eta H_{t-1} = \alpha H_t^d - (\alpha - \eta)H_{t-1} \qquad 3.3$$

where ΔH is the net change in housing stock between times t and $t-1$; H_t^d is the desired stock at time t; H_{t-1} is the actual stock at $t-1$; α is the speed of adjustment ($0 \leqslant \alpha \leqslant 1$); and η is an assumed constant rate of depreciation (net removals). Equation 3.3 implicitly assumes that changes in the level of vacancies are proportional to changes in the desired stock. This relationship is estimated with a cross-section of multifamily housing markets in all the standart metropolitan statistical areas (SMSAs) containing at least a half-million persons in 1970, except Honolulu. There are sixty-four such areas; Honolulu is excluded because of its unusual position as an island community.

The first step in this process is the delineation of the determinants of the desired stock of housing. The structure choice equations (Tables 3-2 to 3-5) provide estimates of the probability of each of several household types choosing apartments. The product of these probabilities (calculated from 1960 data) and the number of households of each type in 1970, when summed over all household types, provides an estimate of the 1970 demand for apartments. That is,

$$HD_{ik} = \sum_j P_{ikj} N_j \qquad \qquad 3.4$$

$$P_{ikj} = f(I, FLC, E, L) \qquad \qquad 3.5$$

where P_{ikj} is the probability of household type j consuming house-type k in residence zone i; HD_{ik} is the number of units of house-type k demanded in zone i; and N_j is the number of households of type j. P_{ikj} is a function of I, FLC, E and L which denote household income, stages in the family life cycle, education of head, and the head's work location. Equations 3.4 and 3.5 predict the demand for various house types in different parts of each metropolitan area.

Tables 3-2 to 3-5 contain estimates of Equation 3.5. However, they cannot be used because there are no 1970 tabulations by SMSA containing all of the 360 cells implied by those equations. Therefore the equations must be reestimated using a different set of categories to describe household characteristics. The revised model is based on a tabulation of SMSA population by marital status and income available for 1960 and 1970. Of course, the deletion of the education and workplace variables, and the less satisfactory description of the family life cycle introduce bias into the estimates of the remaining coefficients. It is hoped that sufficient multicollinearity exists between the included and excluded variables to make the estimates useful for predictive purposes.[15] The revised estimates are computed with ordinary least squares from the same 1960 sample of U.S. households. In order to estimate a full interaction probability function, the large and small SMSAs have been combined. The results are presented in Table 3-6. The intercept represents households with annual incomes of less than $5,000. The coefficient of each income variable is added to the value of the intercept to obtain the probability of a household in that income range selecting an apartment. Household income has a different effect (pattern or size of coefficient) for each family type. Two-person households who are married with spouse present, no nonrelatives and head under forty-five years or forty-five to sixty-four years of age, and two-person households with other male head over sixty-five years of age show the most consistent pattern. As income increases, their probability of selecting an apartment declines, and all the income coefficients are statistically significant at the 5 percent level. For the remaining family types, the probability of selecting an apartment declines as income

Table 3-6
Probability of Selecting Multifamily Housing Stratified by Household Size, Age of Head and Marital Status for Metropolitan Areas of One-half Million or more Persons: 1960[a]

	Intercept	Income $5,000 to $9,999	Income $10,000 to $14,999	Income $15,000 or more	R^2 (Corrected)	F	N
One Person Households							
Under 65	0.5802 (43.9)	0.0210 (0.80)	-0.0995 (-1.43)	-0.0318 (-0.36)	—	1.02	1953
65 or over	0.4490 (26.6)	0.1224 (1.88)	0.0510 (0.32)	0.0964 (0.64)	0.001	1.32	957
Two Person Households Married, Spouse Present, No Nonrelatives							
Under 45	0.3266 (36.2)	-0.1664 (-15.4)	-0.2141 (-14.2)	-0.2379 (-10.7)	0.041	106.9	7464
45-64	0.2560 (21.8)	-0.0875 (-6.27)	-0.1030 (-6.15)	-0.1538 (-7.65)	0.013	23.9	5085
65 or over	0.2396 (17.0)	-0.0494 (-1.98)	-0.0287 (-0.73)	-0.0327 (-0.70)	0.001	1.39	1493
Other Male Head							
Under 65	0.2083 (5.92)	-0.0787 (-1.25)	-0.0083 (-0.09)	-0.2083 (-1.29)	—	0.98	200
65 or over	0.4453 (15.7)	-0.1635 (-4.17)	-0.1716 (-3.10)	-0.2786 (-4.38)	0.035	9.76	717
Female Head							
Under 65	0.3666 (24.0)	-0.0559 (-1.89)	-0.1463 (-2.30)	0.0247 (0.25)	0.004	2.70	1407
65 or over	0.2831 (10.6)	-0.0775 (-1.54)	-0.0498 (-0.59)	0.0502 (0.43)	—	0.97	424

[a]t-statistics in parentheses.

increases until the highest income category, but only one of these income coefficients is statistically significant at the 5 percent level. However, the family-type differentiation captures important variations in the probability of selecting an apartment. This is illustrated by the estimates of the noninteraction probability functions (forcing the income coefficients to be the same for all family types) shown in Table 3-7. Since there are important differences in the income coefficients across family types, it is important to capture these variations by using the full interaction model (Table 3-6) in our calculation of the desired demand for multifamily housing. It is also evident that the larger the household, the less likely it is to choose an apartment, and that the proxy for life cycle does not capture the variations detected by the more complete categorization used in Tables 3-2 to 3-5.

The equations in Table 3-6 give the probability of each of thirty-six household types selecting an apartment. Estimates of the desired demand for apartments relying solely on these probability functions do not capture the variation in housing prices between metropolitan areas. For this reason, the structure choice equations are used to estimate the 1960 demand for apartments for each SMSA (HD_{60}), and the difference between this estimate and the actual number of apartments in each SMSA in 1960 (H_{60}) is regressed on the size (population) of the SMSA in 1960 ($SPOP60$) as a proxy variable for variations in the relative prices of apartments and single-family houses. This model (Equation 3.6) explains 53 percent of the residual demand,

$$H_{60} - HD_{60} = -86220. + 0.07112 \, SPOP60$$
$$(-4.72) \qquad (8.36) \qquad\qquad\qquad 3.6$$

$$R^2 \text{ (Corrected)} = 0.53$$

and the proxy for price is statistically significant at the 5 percent level (t-statistics in parentheses). Although other proxies for price (population per square mile in the SMSA, population per square mile in the central city, median rent in the SMSA, and median property value in the SMSA) do not perform as well, SMSA population leaves much to be desired, which is indicated by a standard error of the estimate that is more than ten times the mean value of the dependent variable.

The desired demand for each SMSA in 1970 (H_{70}^d) is estimated as the sum of (1) the numbers obtained from Equation 3.4 using the tabulations of households by marital status and income for 1970 and the 1960 probabilities in Table 3-6,[16] and (2) the numbers obtained from Equation 3.6 by substituting the population of each SMSA in 1970 for $SPOP60$. These figures are then used to estimate the stock adjustment model. The number of multifamily housing units

Table 3-7

Probability of Selecting Multifamily Housing by Size of the Metropolitan Area, Noninteraction Model: 1960[a]

	Metropolitan Areas of One or more Million Persons	Metropolitan Areas of One-half to One Million Persons
One-Person Households 65 or over	−0.1426 (−7.40)	−0.1291 (−4.37)
Two-Person Households		
Married, Spouse Present, No Nonrelatives		
Under 45	−0.3487 (−27.1)	−0.2619 (−12.9)
45-64	−0.3504 (−25.9)	−0.2914 (−13.6)
65 or over	−0.3401 (−20.2)	−0.3115 (−12.2)
Other Male Head		
Under 65	−0.2083 (−9.85)	−0.2015 (−5.82)
65 or over	−0.4378 (−11.8)	−0.1988 (−3.88)
Female Head		
Under 65	−0.2364 (−13.9)	−0.1943 (−7.35)
65 or over	−0.2996 (−11.5)	−0.3168 (−8.01)
Income $5,000 to $9,999	−0.1125 (−13.0)	−0.0788 (−6.36)
Income $10,000 to $14,999	−0.1469 (−12.2)	−0.1318 (−6.74)
Income $15,000 or more	−0.1845 (−11.8)	−0.1085 (−3.97)
Intercept	0.6570 (59.0)	0.4503 (25.1)
R^2 (Corrected)	0.11	0.08
F	165.6	39.0
N	15,121	4,579

[a]t-statistics in parentheses.

in each of the sixty-four SMSAs in 1960 constitutes the actual stock at the beginning of the period, and the net change in that stock in the decade is the dependent variable. Equation 3.7 is an estimate of the stock adjustment model for the 1960-70 period (t-statistics in parentheses).

$$H_{60-70} = 17360. + 0.2992\,H_{70}^{d} - 0.1550\,H_{60}$$
$$\phantom{H_{60-70} = 17360.} (4.79) \quad (10.5) \qquad (-5.53) \qquad\qquad 3.7$$

$$R^2 \text{ (Corrected)} = 0.77$$

All the variables have the correct sign and are statistically significant at the 0.1 percent level. The larger the 1970 demand (H_{70}^{d}) for multifamily housing, the larger the increase in the stock since 1960. The 1960 stock of multifamily housing restrained the additions; those SMSAs with the larger stocks had smaller changes in the decade. According to Equation 3.7, the housing market adds 29.9 percent of the *decade* excess of desired over actual stock during one period (decade), and the rate of replacement (η) is estimated to be 14.4 percent for a ten-year period (0.2992 minus 0.1550). Muth's estimate of the coefficient of stock adjustment using annual data is that 31.7 percent of the *annual* excess of desired over actual stock is added during one year.[17] Muth's annual estimate can be compared to the present ten-year estimate by applying Muth's annual coefficient of adjustment to an annual excess of desired over actual stock for each of the ten years until the end of the decade. That is, the excess of desired over actual stock for the first year has ten years to adjust; that for the second year has nine years to adjust; and so forth. The fraction of each year's excess of desired over actual stock that has been supplied by the end of the decade is calculated.[18] When the ten fractions are added and divided by 10, the *ten-year* coefficient of adjustment implied by the annual one is obtained. For Muth's annual coefficient of 31.7 percent, the implied ten-year coefficient is 69.2 percent which is more than two times as large as the 29.9 percent estimated in Equation 3.7. The annual coefficient implied by a ten-year coefficient of 29.9 percent is about 8 percent, or roughly one-fourth Muth's annual coefficient.

Since Equation 3.6 is an unsatisfactory model of the influence of price differentials, the stock adjustment model is also estimated without trying to introduce price variations. That is, the desired demand variable is the number of households likely to demand apartments as predicted from Equation 3.4 using 1970 tabulations of households by marital status and income and the 1960 probabilities in Table 3-6. Equation 3.8 is the estimate of this version of the stock adjustment model where HP_{70}^{d} is used to distinguish this desired demand variable from the one in Equation 3.7. Both variables in Equation 3.8 have the correct signs and are statistically significant at the 0.1 percent level.

$$H_{60\text{-}70} = -8398. + 0.6044\, HP_{70}^{d} - 0.1810\, H_{60}$$
$$(-1.78) \quad (11.4) \quad\quad (-6.43) \quad\quad\quad\quad 3.8$$

R^2 (Corrected) $= 0.80$

As in Equation 3.7, the larger the desired demand, the larger the increase in the stock since 1960, and those SMSAs with the larger stocks at the start of the period add fewer units during the decade. The R^2 is 3 percent larger. However, the ten-year coefficient of stock adjustment is 60.4 percent and relatively close to the ten-year coefficient implied by Muth's annual value. The coefficient of replacement is 42.3 percent for ten years, or 4.23 percent per year, which implies that multifamily housing units have a rather short life of twenty-five years.

Since Equations 3.7 and 3.8 have standard errors of the estimate that are 57 and 54 percent, respectively, of the mean value of the dependent variable, neither equation has the accuracy desired for predictive purposes. This is further illustrated in Table 3-8 by the comparison of the actual and predicted values of the dependent variable (net change in multifamily housing over 1960-70) for Equation 3.8. A fully specified Equation 3.5 would have probably produced better results. As between the two versions of the stock adjustment model estimated here, I would choose Equation 3.8 over Equation 3.7 on the basis of the estimate of the coefficient of stock adjustment. The 1/100 samples of the population of SMSAs in the 1970 census contain the information that is needed to construct the tabulations of households by stage in the family life cycle, income, and workplace. Variations in the relative prices of multifamily and single-family housing could also be included directly in the demand functions estimated from these 1970 samples for use in projecting future demands. These samples should greatly improve the quality of housing market studies and projections.

Summary

The effect of lower commuting costs and rising family incomes on urban form and development has received widespread recognition, while the implications of variations in the distribution of population characteristics on the nature of urban areas have received much less attention. However, substantial movement in the age distribution of the population in the last twenty years has contributed to a reversal of the long-term trend toward lower density urban development. Although the boom in multifamily housing, which accompanied the changes in the age distribution of the population, has increased net residential density, most of the new multifamily housing is less dense than older multifamily housing.

Table 3-8

Actual and Estimated Net Change in Multifamily Housing Units for Sixty-four SMSAs: 1960-70

Observation (SMSA)	Actual Value	Estimated Value	Residual	Percent Error
Akron	12,482	15,940	−3,458	27.7
Albany-Schenectady-Troy	9,610	17,554	−7,944	82.7
Allentown-Bethlehem-Easton	10,383	12,486	−2,103	20.3
Anaheim-Santa Ana-Garden Grove	92,368	43,084	49,284	53.4
Atlanta	72,977	39,954	33,022	45.2
Baltimore	67,742	66,325	1,417	2.1
Birmingham	8,283	21,901	−13,618	164.4
Boston	54,620	67,325	−12,705	23.3
Buffalo	4,259	37,952	−33,693	791.1
Chicago	135,100	161,230	−26,134	19.3
Cincinnati	27,787	36,566	−8,779	31.6
Cleveland	52,353	60,807	−8,454	16.1
Columbus, Ohio	30,900	24,917	5,983	19.4
Dallas	79,874	51,825	28,049	35.1
Dayton	20,229	21,831	−1,602	7.9
Denver	39,541	37,329	2,212	5.6
Detroit	72,506	132,270	−59,768	82.4
Fort Lauderdale-Hollywood	55,858	21,354	34,504	61.8
Fort Worth	24,493	21,424	3,069	12.5
Gary-Hammond-East Chicago	6,073	10,264	−4,191	69.0
Grand Rapids	6,744	11,286	−4,542	67.3
Greensboro-Winston Salem-High Point	9,123	15,096	−5,973	65.5
Hartford	19,380	10,429	8,951	46.2
Houston	89,976	67,628	22,348	24.8
Indianapolis	33,710	32,888	822	2.4
Jacksonville, Florida	10,574	12,925	−2,171	20.2
Jersey City	10,710	3,482	7,228	67.5
Kansas City	18,749	36,696	−17,947	95.7
Los Angeles-Long Beach	318,860	254,040	64,827	20.3
Louisville	19,229	21,852	−2,623	13.6

Table 3-8 (cont.)

Observation (SMSA)	Actual Value	Estimated Value	Residual	Percent Error
Memphis	21,459	20,229	1,230	5.7
Miami	65,477	39,768	25,708	39.3
Milwaukee	27,299	39,099	−11,800	43.2
Minneapolis-St. Paul	60,451	52,391	8,060	13.3
Nashville-Davidson	15,296	12,835	2,461	16.1
New Orleans	14,898	29,075	−14,177	95.2
New York	198,380	201,870	−3,491	1.8
Newark	46,784	40,438	6,346	13.6
Norfolk-Portsmouth	14,059	13,682	377	2.7
Oklahoma City	14,714	19,244	−4,530	30.8
Omaha	12,318	10,656	1,662	13.5
Patterson-Clifton-Passaic	35,346	33,302	2,044	5.8
Philadelphia	126,120	169,670	−43,549	34.5
Phoenix	35,664	30,972	4,692	13.2
Pittsburgh	35,467	80,755	−45,288	127.7
Portland, Oregon	24,609	34,457	9,849	40.0
Providence-Pawtucket-Warwick	9,793	18,436	−8,643	88.3
Richmond	18,308	11,810	6,498	35.5
Rochester	22,599	21,946	653	2.9
Sacramento	25,781	23,832	1,949	7.6
St. Louis	37,313	71,965	−34,652	92.9
Salt Lake City	9,224	9,790	−566	6.1
San Antonio	18,986	23,910	−4,924	25.9
San Bernardino-Riverside-Ontario	31,372	40,915	−9,543	30.4
San Diego	45,606	44,621	985	2.2
San Francisco-Oakland	103,110	111,330	−8,219	8.0
San Jose	57,123	29,034	28,089	49.2
Seattle-Everett	41,855	45,443	−3,588	8.6
Springfield-Chicopee-Holyoke	5,856	7,325	−1,469	25.1
Syracuse	13,272	13,586	−314	2.4
Tampa-St. Petersburg	23,611	44,421	−20,810	88.1
Toledo	11,363	17,551	−6,188	54.3
Washington, D.C.	178,280	78,388	99,873	56.0
Youngstown-Warren	6,159	11,216	−5,057	82.1

That is, within the multifamily housing submarket, a trend toward lower density structures is discernible.

Closer examination of the structure-type choices of households shows that stages in the family life cycle provide a powerful description of the propensity to select an apartment and one more meaningful than age of head and family size which have been widely used. Young, unmarried households are most likely to select an apartment; married households with the youngest child over six and head thirty to sixty years old and married households with children and head over sixty years old are least likely to select an apartment. The probability of selecting an apartment increases for households over sixty years old if they are either married without children at home or widowed. The higher the family income, the lower the probability of selecting an apartment, but the effect of income on structure choice varies by stage in the family life cycle. Income has the strongest effect among married households, especially those with children. Whether or not the head is college-educated has only a weak effect on structure choice; those with a college education are slightly more likely to select an apartment. In general, households with heads working in the center of a metropolitan area are more likely to live in apartments than households whose heads work in the suburbs. However, the effect of workplace on structure choice varies by stage in the family life cycle; households with children present are affected least, and those that are single, divorced, separated, or widowed are affected most.

Household preferences for suburban apartments are also examined with results paralleling those for apartments regardless of their location. One notable difference is that the probability of selecting a suburban apartment is less than that of selecting an apartment or that of selecting a central city apartment. The preference functions for suburban apartments also confirm the hypothesis, developed in Chapter 2, that the construction of apartments in the suburbs has been in part the result of the suburbanization of employment. Suburban workers are more likely to select a suburban apartment than central city workers.

4

The Spatial Distribution of Multifamily Housing

Suburban Apartments

Over half the multifamily housing units constructed in metropolitan areas in the 1960s have been built in the suburbs (see Chapter 2). This section develops an aggregate model that describes the forces affecting the distribution of population between the central city and its suburban ring by drawing upon the work of John Neidercorn and John Kain.[1] Their econometric model of metropolitan development falls within the framework outlined in Chapter 2; it can be divided into two parts. The first part explains changes in metropolitan (SMSA) population in terms of the rate of growth of SMSA manufacturing employment, a proxy for "basic" employment. The age of the central city also enters this relationship; it captures the slower rate of population growth observed in older areas. The second part of the model determines central city and suburban population and manufacturing, retailing, wholesaling, and service employment. The following equations illustrate the second part of their model.

$$\Delta M_c = \alpha_{71} \, V \Delta M_s^g + \alpha_{72} \Delta M_s^d + \alpha_{73} \qquad \text{4.1}$$

$$\Delta P_c = \alpha_{81} \, V \Delta P_s + \alpha_{82} \Delta M_c + \alpha_{83} \qquad \text{4.2}$$

$$\Delta M_r = \Delta M_s - \Delta M_c \qquad \text{4.3}$$

$$\Delta P_r = \Delta P_s - \Delta P_c \qquad \text{4.4}$$

where M is manufacturing employment; P is population; V is the fraction of the central city's land area which is vacant. The subscripts c, r, and s refer to the central city, suburban ring, and the entire SMSA. The Δ's refer to changes over a time period. And

$$\Delta M_s^g = \begin{cases} \Delta M_s \text{ if } \Delta M_s > 0 \\ 0 \text{ if } \Delta M_s \leqslant 0 \end{cases}$$

$$\Delta M_s^d = \begin{cases} \Delta M_s \text{ if } \Delta M_s < 0 \\ 0 \text{ if } \Delta M_s \geqslant 0 \end{cases}$$

59

According to this model, central city manufacturing employment changes depend on the change in SMSA manufacturing employment. If manufacturing employment increases in the SMSA, the central city's share of this growth is constrained by the availability of vacant land suitable for modern plant construction. When SMSA manufacturing employment is declining, vacant land in the central city does not influence the pattern of behavior. Vacant land restricts manufacturing employment (and population) growth in the central city for three reasons. First, if vacant land has disappeared, land already in use must be used more intensively, which requires demolition thus increasing costs.[2] Second, the high-rise structures that constitute more intensive use are not suitable for modern day plant technology which requires a smooth flow of materials. (In the case of residential use, a limited supply of vacant land restricts the city's capacity to compete for the many households desiring lower density living arrangements than are generally available in central cities.) Third, central cities have been reclaiming land to increase the amount of open space, thus removing land from manufacturing (and residential) use.

Changes in central city population are tied to changes in central city manufacturing employment and to changes in SMSA population constrained by the vacant land ratio. (SMSA population is not divided into growing and declining SMSAs because only one of the SMSAs investigated by Niedercorn and Kain experienced a decline.) The last two equations close the system. Neidercorn and Kain estimated their model on a cross-section of the thirty-nine largest SMSAs during the 1954-58 period. They found that

only a very small part of the total SMSA population increment settles in the Central City. If the vacant land ratio is 0.10, only 4 percent find homes there. However, each increment or decrement of Central City manufacturing employment induces a Central City population change of 0.82 persons. Evidently, people move to remain near their jobs. Also, there is a strong tendency (about 2,000 people per year) to leave the Central City, as indicated by the negative intercept. Many families move to the suburbs when it becomes financially possible, thus indicating a preference for low-density dwelling. This is perhaps the strongest reason for pessimism about future Central City growth.[3]

The probability models of Chapter 3 (Tables 3-2 to 3-5) indicate that shifts of employment to the suburbs will increase the demand for suburban apartments. That analysis in combination with Neidercorn and Kain's suggest that the distribution of new apartments between the ring and the central city should be related to changes in the location of employment. It should also be related to the normal growth of the population resident at the beginning of the period. In addition, older central cities, at least during the 1950s, are likely to have had an excess supply of apartments due to wartime controls and the shift in preferences accompanying higher incomes and more mobility (see Chapter 2 for a more detailed discussion). Such an excess supply would tend to restrict activity in a suburban apartment market. As the quality of the central city stock declines, particularly the quality of neighborhoods and public services, these central city apartments would no longer be able to compete with new apartment construction in the suburbs. Consequently, excess central city supplies probably restricted suburban apartment development during most of the 1950s but were either less related or not at all related to suburban apartment activity in the 1960s. Equation 4.5 represents a simple model designed to capture these three effects, which also fits within the framework of the Neidercorn-Kain model.

$$\Delta MH_r = \beta_0 + \beta_1 \Delta E_r + \beta_2 \Delta P_r + \beta_3 A \qquad 4.5$$

where ΔMH_r is the annual net change over a decade in the stock of multifamily housing units (units in buildings with three or more units); A is the age of the central city measured in terms of the number of years since the central city reached one-half its population at the beginning of the period; ΔE_r is the annual change in total employment in the ring, and ΔP_r is the annual change in the ring's population. This model is estimated for two decades: 1950-60 and 1960-70. Total employment consists of manufacturing, wholesaling, retailing, and selected services as reported in the 1954, 1958, 1963, and 1967 *Census of Manufactures* and *Census of Business* (see Table 2-3). The annual changes in multifamily housing and in population are calculated from the 1950, 1960, and 1970 *Census of Housing* and *Census of Population*.[4]

The 1960 definitions of SMSAs and central cities are used for the 1950-60 period, and the 1970 definitions are used for 1960-70. This insures constant boundaries for the annual changes in population. Since annual changes in multifamily housing could not be corrected for boundary changes, the percentage of the SMSA population annexed to the central city during the decade (*PPA*) is included as a control variable.[5] However, this variable does not account for alterations in the SMSA boundaries; in some cases (Los Angeles-Long Beach and Anaheim-Santa Ana-Garden Grove) exact corrections are possible. In most cases, changes in the definition of SMSA are likely to add areas that were largely undeveloped at the beginning of the period and probably contained few, if any, apartments at that time. Consequently, these changes are not likely to create a serious estimation problem. The model is estimated for most of the SMSAs analyzed earlier in Chapter 3.[6]

It is hoped that the age variable will detect the excess supply of central city multifamily housing in the 1950s (a negative sign) and the growing obsolescence of this stock during the 1960s (a positive sign). However, the age variable is ambiguous because it includes both forces in both time periods and probably represents some other restrictions such as the availability of vacant land in the central city and differentials in replacement demand arising from demolitions. Therefore the model is estimated on a subsample for which vacant land data is available; the fraction of the central city's land area which is vacant (V) is included as a variable.[7] The age variable can at most suggest which force dominates. The estimates of three formulations for each decade are summarized in Table 4-1. All versions provide reasonably good fits: 63 percent of the variation is explained for 1950-60 and 76 percent for 1960-70. The changes in ring population and employment have positive effects and are statistically significant at the 5 percent level for 1950-60. Although both have positive signs in 1960-70, only the change in ring population is statistically significant. However, multicollinearity is more pervasive in the second period; for the 1950-60 period, the determinants of the correlation matrix are roughly three times as large as those for 1960-70. In addition, Bartlet's chi-square test more clearly rejects the hypothesis that the independent variables are orthogonal for 1960-70 than for 1950-60. Examination of the other statistics suggested by Farrar and Glauber indicates the presence of multicollinearity in both periods with the recent one most burdened by the problem.[8] Therefore low t-statistics cannot be relied upon for hypothesis testing. The estimates of the coefficients are still unbiased although they are less precise; that is, their probability distributions are flatter.

Table 4-1

The Determinants of Multifamily Housing Construction in the Suburban Rings of Selected SMSAs: 1950-60 and 1960-70[a]

	1950-1960			1960-1970		
Change in Total Ring Employment	0.001341 (2.73)	0.001363 (2.73)	0.001348 (2.50)	0.05256 (0.91)	0.04284 (0.74)	0.05336 (0.84)
Change in Ring Population	0.03576 (7.25)	0.03515 (6.70)	0.03503 (5.84)	0.1281 (6.03)	0.1374 (6.26)	0.1303 (5.18)
Age of Central City	−15.69 (−1.60)	−17.77 (−1.56)	−20.82 (−1.53)	3.961 (0.35)	9.579 (0.82)	7.125 (0.54)
PPA	−	−387.6 (−0.36)	−530.9 (−0.44)	−	5904. (1.48)	5513. (1.20)
V	−	−	−0.9371 (−0.04)	−	−	−22.27 (−0.97)
Intercept	203.5 (0.48)	333.8 (0.60)	475.5 (0.67)	−355.2 (−0.61)	−938.0 (−1.35)	−937.5 (−1.19)
R^2 (Corrected)	0.63	0.63	0.61	0.76	0.76	0.75
N	57	57	50	61	61	54
Determinant of the Correlation Matrix	0.79	0.53	0.46	0.23	0.18	0.17
Bartlet's Chi-Square Test of Orthogonality (and Degrees of Freedom)	12.8(3)	34.3(6)	37.2(10)	86.2(3)	100.5(6)	91.6(10)

[a]t-statistics in parentheses.

The models indicate that an annual increase of 1,000 suburban jobs produced 1.3 suburban apartments annually in the 1950s and 52 suburban apartments annually in the 1960s. The employment effect is much stronger in the second period, and so is the population effect. An annual increase of 1,000 persons in the suburban population produced only 35 suburban apartments annually in the first period but 128 in the second period.

The age of the central city has a negative coefficient in the 1950s and a positive one in the 1960s. During the 1950s, the market for suburban apartments was smaller in SMSAs with older central cities, a result consistent with the hypothesis of an excess supply of central city apartments due to shifts in employment location and postwar prosperity. During the 1960s, these same cities have had a larger market for suburban apartments than SMSAs with newer central cities, indicating that the stock of apartments in the older central cities was growing obsolescent and becoming less able to compete with new suburban construction. Although the age variable is not an ideal proxy, it does pick up the effects which a priori reasoning strongly suggested. Additional evidence on the growing obsolescence of the central city stock will be presented below.

The vacant land variable has the expected sign indicating the larger the central city's vacant land supply, the smaller the market for suburban apartments in both periods. Since the Farrar-Glauber tests on the auxiliary regressions indicated that the vacant land variable was orthogonal to the others in both periods, its t-statistic is a reliable indication that vacant land is not statistically significant at the 5 percent level.

Housing Abandonment in the Central City

If the stock of central city apartments, especially in cities with a sizeable 1950 stock, has been growing obsolescent and becoming less able to compete with new suburban apartments, some central city apartments should be leaving the market. It is important to review the nature of the obsolescence of this stock, which is closely tied to housing attributes over which the owner of a structure has little or no control, in particular neighborhood quality and the level of public services. As households become better off, they demand a higher quality environment (neighborhood and public services) as well as structure. It is important to note that this improvement in the welfare of households need not lead to a change in their welfare relative to all other households. Households need only have more resources today than they had yesterday. That real per capita, disposable personal income has increased every year since 1958 is evidence that household well-being has improved in this sense. The standing stock of dwellings, their spatial distribution, and spatial variations in the quality of neighborhood and public services limit the ability of certain portions of metropolitan areas to satisfy this demand. As a result, structures being vacated or abandoned may often be in better condition than occupied structures of the same type located in other parts of the city.

Although it is difficult to quantify the extent of abandonment, many analysts, local, state, and national officials have been pointing to its widespread existence since 1971. Chicago, Cleveland, Detroit, Hoboken, Philadelphia, and St. Louis are cities containing sizeable numbers of abandoned dwelling units.[9] Population changes are indicative of the changing character of demand for housing in these central cities. According to the *1970 Census of Population*, the population of each of these cities (defined in terms of their 1960 boundaries) has declined during the 1960s.[10] St. Louis, which is reported to be the city experiencing the highest degree of abandonment, has also undergone one of the largest percentage declines in population.

Rental vacancy rates in central cities and their suburban rings provide some additional evidence on the relative competitiveness of the central city stock. These rates are available for the years since 1965, with quarterly data since 1969, and are summarized in Table 4-2. The central-city rental vacancy rate has been consistently higher than the suburban one. Except for a few quarters, the two rates have been moving further apart. In addition, more than half the vacant rental units have been in older buildings which have a higher probability of being located in low-quality neighborhoods than newer buildings. Again, this information is not proof of the hypothesis that the central-city apartment stock has moved from an excess supply competitive with suburban apartments to one uncompetitive. However, it is another piece of evidence consistent with the hypothesis. And consistency between theory and data is all that one can hope for; the greater the consistency, the more confidence the theory deserves.

Summary

The hypothesis relating suburban apartments and suburban employment is also confirmed by separate estimates of a model of the suburbanization of apartments for each of the last two census decades. For every 1000 new suburban jobs, fifty-two new suburban apartments were constructed during the 1960s. The same model also lends credence to the hypothesis that an excess supply of high-quality multifamily housing in the early 1950s retarded the suburbanization of apartments and that the growing obsolescence of central-city multifamily housing during the 1960s fostered the development of suburban apartments.

Table 4-2
Rental Vacancy Rates in United States Central Cities and Suburban Rings:
1965-72

Year	Quarter	Central Cities	Suburban Ring	Percent of Vacant U.S. Rental Units in Buildings Built Before 1940
1965	–	7.4	7.4	58
1966	–	6.5	6.4	57
1967	–	5.7	5.2	58
1968	–	5.1	4.2	60
1969	III	4.8	3.9	57
1969	IV	4.8	3.4	56
1970	I	4.9	4.4	56
1970	II	4.8	4.3	56
1970	III	5.0	3.7	56
1970	IV	5.1	3.8	55
1971	I	4.9	4.5	55
1971	II	5.1	3.9	54
1971	III	5.2	4.7	53
1971	IV	5.2	4.6	52
1972	I	5.1	5.0	52
1972	II	5.8	4.6	51
1972	III	5.9	5.5	51
1972	IV	6.2	4.2	52

Source: U.S. Bureau of the Census, *Current Housing Reports. Housing Vacancies.* Series H-111, Nos. 62 to 72-4 (December 1970 to February 1973) (Washington, D.C.: Government Printing Office), Tables 2, 3 and 4.

5

Hedonic Price Indexes: An Econometric Analysis of the Dimensions of the Multifamily Housing Bundle

Housing market analysis has traditionally focused on dwelling units by implicitly or explicitly assuming that these are homogeneous units of measurement. In fact, dwelling units differ widely in structure attributes (internal and external, including lot size) and neighborhood attributes (public and private). It is these attributes, or more accurately combinations of them, that households demand. Housing market analysis faces very difficult measurement problems because the number of attributes is very large, many are difficult to quantify, and even those that are quantifiable are often not quantifiable in comparable terms. Some simplifications are prerequisite to any meaningful analysis. Unless the most important attributes are isolated and means of comparing them developed, the numbers of different bundles of attributes and therefore different commodities would be so large that nothing beyond observing the existence of the bundle would be possible.

The concept of housing attributes, which parallels the work of Lancaster, suggests that housing expenditures (R) be viewed as a function of the prices (P) and quantity (Q) of the attributes composing a particular bundle.[1]

$$R_i = f(P_{1i}, \ldots, P_{ni}, Q_{1i}, \ldots, Q_{ni})$$ 5.1

where n is the number of attributes in the ith bundle. Although different combinations of attributes can produce the same total expenditure, this is equally true of "goods" such as clothing and food appearing in consumer price indexes and household budget analyses. The total amount spent on a good does not allow us to distinguish what was purchased. In the case of housing, as in the case of food or clothing, each attribute's prices and quantity must be known before the actual consumption patterns of different households can be separated. Only then can the bundle be identified. The major difference between housing and these other goods is that the individual attributes of housing cannot be purchased separately.

Equation 5.1, as it now stands, cannot be used to study the behavior of housing markets because (1) the prices of individual attributes are unobserved; (2) the quantities of individual attributes are difficult or impossible to measure; and (3) interdependencies pervade the housing market. The last point means that the purchase of a certain amount of the kth attribute, which was desired, may force the consumption of an amount of the lth attribute, which was not desired. This would be true of many goods under Lancaster's formulation, even though they are considered to have separate identity in today's market place. For example, everyone knows what an apple is but it has several attributes (taste, odor, texture, etc.) and its purchase for any one attribute buys all the others.

If, however, attribute prices could be *imputed* through data on a variety of attribute bundles, then Equation 5.1 could be utilized to price various bundles. Suppliers of housing services might be able to use such information to assess the probability of profiting from the production of certain bundles, especially if the specification of the model accounts for interdependencies.

Since housing is a durable good, its prices may include quasi rents which appear because of supply inelasticity in the short run. According to Stigler:

A quasi-rent is the return to a durable specific productive instrument. If the productive factor is durable, it will be used throughout its life provided it yields more than its scrap value. Since it is a concrete productive instrument, say a house or machine tool, it is specialized to some degree, and cannot change into another form if the demand for its services falls. In the long run—in a period long enough to build new instruments or wear out old ones—the return to the instrument must equal the current rate of return on capital (with appropriate allowance for risk). If the machine's quasi-rents are less than interest plus depreciation, it will not be replaced; if the quasi-rents exceed interest plus depreciation, more will be built until equilibrium is restored. The long-run *net* return on capital goods must yield the appropriate interest rate; their short-run *gross* return is a quasi-rent.[2]

Quasi rents exist because of mistaken expectations at the time of investment about future supply and demand for the services flowing from the attributes of a house. If the demand for the bundles of attributes capable of being provided from a given structure falls, the quasi rents will not return the investment plus the expected rate of return. The durability of structures coupled with the spatial distribution of structural and neighborhood attributes suggests that these quasi rents should vary spatially. Some of the more important neighborhood attributes are the quality and quantity of local governmental services (e.g., schools, garbage collection, police and fire protection, and snow removal), the quality of adjacent structures, the density and physical arrangement of the neighborhood and the characteristics of neighbors (e.g., income, education, age, and occupation). In addition, the interdependencies of housing attributes, which result in large part from the historical pattern of development, reinforce a spatial distribution for quasi rents. Each attribute could conceivably have a spatial quasi rent included in its price. This is represented in Equation 5.2.

$$R_i = f(p_{1i} + r_{1i}, \ldots, p_{ni} + r_{ni}, Q_{1i}, \ldots, Q_{ni}) \qquad 5.2$$

where r_{ji} is the spatial quasi rent for the jth attribute in the ith bundle, p_{ji} is the market price of the jth attribute in the ith bundle which does not vary spatially, and P_{ji} is the sum of p_{ji} and r_{ji}. (The i subscript can be deleted from p_{ji} if it is assumed that the attribute price is not bundle specific.) When a particular attribute is being produced at a certain location, then p_j is equal to the average variable unit cost of production. As John Kain and John Quigley point out, the market value of an attribute currently being produced (or created) must equal or exceed p_j.[3] However, this need only hold for those locations where it is currently in production. In fact, the same attribute could have positive quasi rents at some locations (places of production) and negative ones at others. Negative quasi rents would result from a decline in demand for an attribute at a certain location (two-family houses on 4000 square feet lots in the central city) combined with a stock that cannot be profitably transformed to meet current demands (single-family houses on 7000 square feet lots).

The hedonic price technique has been used to analyze several other commodities which have some of the difficulties associated with housing. In an investigation of quality change in automobiles, Zvi Griliches notes that

only a few of the observed quality changes come in discrete lumps with an attached price (automatic transmissions). Most of the changes are gradual and are not priced separately. Nevertheless, many dimensions of quality change can be quantified ...; a variety of models with different specifications can be observed being sold at different prices at the same time; using multiple regression techniques on these data one can derive implicit prices per unit of the chosen additional dimension of the commodity.[4]

Housing attributes, which vary gradually across the stock and its spatial distribution, are not priced separately. In addition to deriving implicit prices for attributes, this technique lends itself to pricing a bundle of attributes at geographical locations where it is not available, and provides a better basis for isolating the attributes which appear to be most important. Estimation of Equation 5.2 for each submarket does not necessarily require the attributes to have a numerical quantification; with sufficient observations, "dummy" variables, which take a value of one if a particular bundle possesses a particular attribute and zero if it does not, can be utilized. A "dummy" variable provides an estimate of the average contribution of its attribute to the price of the bundle in that submarket. Many important attributes, which are elusive and difficult to measure, can be approximated by some measure with which they are well correlated; such "proxy" variables will prove valuable in efforts to capture neighborhood attributes.

There are three basic aspects to Equation 5.2: (1) structural attributes, (2) neighborhood attributes, and (3) quasi rents. We must make assumptions about the form of the relationship and the attributes to be included in the index. Theory does not help us answer either of these questions. In some sense, they are empirical questions. There is no a priori reason to expect any given form of relationship between bundle price and bundle attributes. Although Griliches used the semilogorithmic form, relating the logarithm of bundle price to its attributes, he notes that "there is no a priori reason to expect price and quality to be related in any particular fixed fashion,"[5] and points out that other forms, linear or log-log, may be more appropriate for other commodities. In this chapter, a hedonic price index is estimated for two-bedroom apartments in new (post-1960) multifamily (five or more units per building) rental housing in the greater Boston area.

The Sample and the Variables

Seventy-six apartment developments in the greater Boston area, all of which were constructed in the 1960s and probably since 1965, were surveyed in the months of December 1972 and January 1973. Information was gathered on the presence of various attributes inside apartments (e.g., dishwashers, disposals, airconditioners) in these developments and on the attributes (e.g., swimming pools, tennis courts) provided by the development. Each development was assessed for the view it offered its residents: a panoramic view of surrounding land or water was rated excellent; a view of woods or landscaped grounds was rated pleasant; and developments with a low quality view and/or environment such as major highways or shopping centers were described as having "yucky" views. Each of these variables has a value of one if the attribute was present and zero if it was not. Neighborhood attributes are represented by the view variables and by census statistics on density, age of dwelling units, and median income.

The bundle price is the monthly rent of a two-bedroom apartment which consisted of a kitchen, living room, dining area (usually part of the living room), two bedrooms, and one and one-half bathrooms, or the nearest equivalent in a development. (Several developments offer only one-bath, two-bedroom units or two-bath, two-bedroom units.) Rents also tend to vary with elevation above the ground; the standard unit was defined as being on the second floor except in the case of town-house apartments and high-rise buildings. Town-house apartments have a ground floor and a second floor within the same unit. High-rise buildings usually offer a view which is only available from the upper floors; the rent of a tenth-floor apartment was used to capture this amenity. When identical units on the same floor had different rents depending on their location (corner, interior wall, or exterior wall), the rent on a corner unit was used as the measure of bundle price.

Measurement of the Attributes

The survey provided information on thirty-six interior and exterior attributes of each development. The three view variables, only two of which can enter the hedonic price equation because they are mutually exclusive categories, are treated as representing neighborhood attributes. Since there are so few measures of neighborhood attributes, view is analyzed separately from the remaining thirty-three attributes. If each of these variables were included in the regression, the loss in degrees of freedom would have been costly with the small sample. Furthermore, it is quite possible that consumers and the market evaluate bundles of attributes in terms of a few broad aggregates. John Kain and John Quigley found that thirty-nine measures of the physical or visual quality of the bundle of residential services in their study of St. Louis could be combined into five composite quality variables that seemed to represent separable and intuitively meaningful quality dimensions (the exterior physical environment; structural condition and housekeeping inside the unit; cleanliness, landscaping, and condition of nearby properties; the presence and effect of commercial and industrial land uses; and the average quality of structures on the block face as a whole).[6] These five composite variables were produced by factor analysis and explained 60 percent of the variance among the thirty-nine original variables; they also performed well in their efforts to estimate the market value of specific attributes.

Factor analysis is used in the present study to aggregate the thirty-three attributes into a few composite measures of bundle attributes. In order to obtain solutions, one of the thirty-three (air-conditioning) had to be deleted because of its high correlation (0.736) with another attribute (garbage disposals). In only one case do these two variables take on a different value. Three-, four-, and five-factor solutions were attempted. The three-factor solution yields the most meaningful results and is summarized in Table 5-1. These factors are calculated by rotating the factor matrix. They load on only twenty of the thirty-two individual attributes. (Kain and Quigley's five-factor solution, which appears to have been calculated without rotation, loaded on thirty-three of their thirty-nine variables.) The first factor loads heavily on ten attributes describing adult recreation facilities. The second factor represents security; two of the four attributes with loadings greater than 0.4 involve management's direct efforts to protect occupants, and the other two (elevator and covered parking) have indirect implications for tenant protection. The third factor loads on eight attributes and describes the development's attractiveness to families with children; the outdoor recreation attributes included in this variable are likely to be highly used by children or families with children. Each factor represents an intuitively sensible composite measure that households could be expected to value.

Neighborhood attributes are represented by the view variables and the characteristics of the census tract (town in the case of areas not tracted by the Bureau of the Census) in which the development is located. Three census variables were tried: the fraction of the tract's housing units which are single-family; the fraction of the tract's housing units which were constructed

Table 5-1
Factor Loadings on Individual Attributes

Attributes	Factor[a]		
	1	2	3
Elevator	*	0.66	*
Covered Parking	*	0.68	*
Security Guards (Not Necessarily Uniformed)	*	0.64	*
Gatehouse for security	*	0.53	*
Closed Circuit TV or Intercom	*	*	*
Exercise Rooms and Equipment	0.69	0.50	*
Sauna	0.60	0.52	*
Billiards	0.63	*	*
Shuffleboard	0.76	*	*
Handball or Squash	0.72	*	*
Function Room(s) (e.g., Party or Card Rooms)	0.51	*	0.48
Arts and Crafts Studio(s)	0.42	*	*
Woodworking Shop	0.59	*	*
Social Director	0.82	*	*
Natural Ice Skating Rink	*	*	*
Lake	*	*	*
Putting Green	*	*	*
Basketball Court(s)	0.40	*	0.56
Tennis Court(s)	*	*	0.53
Swimming Pool	*	*	0.46
Baseball Diamond(s)	*	*	0.54
Picnic Area	*	*	0.49
Playground	*	*	0.51
Kindergarten, Daycare, or Babysitting service	*	*	0.60
Private Storage Space	*	*	*
24-hour Maintenance Service	*	*	*
Laundry Facilities	*	*	*
Dishwasher	*	*	*
Garbage Disposal	*	*	*
Private Balcony or Patio	*	*	*
Wooded Grounds	*	*	*
Private Garden Plots	*	*	*

[a]An * indicates a factor loading less than 0.40.

before 1940; and the median income of the families and unrelated individuals residing in the tract in 1970. These census descriptions have been used with success by William Apgar and John Kain in a study of Pittsburgh's housing market that investigated the ability of census tract data to characterize differences in neighborhood attributes.[7] Unfortunately these three measures are highly correlated (0.48 or more in magnitude) with one another in the present sample, and the inclusion of all three measures in a regression leads to nonsensical results. When each variable is entered separately in the regression equations, it performs as expected: the density measure has a positive relationship, the age variable a negative relationship, and the income measure a positive relationship with the bundle price. However, the median income measure is the best proxy of neighborhood attributes, and it is used in the equations reported here. Since the Boston metropolitan area is divided into over 100 small cities and towns, the regressions have also been estimated using measures of density, age, and income computed on the basis of the whole town except in the case of the city of Boston. These town-based measures do not perform as well as those measured at the census tract level, which illustrates the importance of obtaining measures of the attributes of the immediate area around a development. Census tract measures are used in this study, but they may even cover too large an area. In addition, apartment developments are often located on the borders of census tracts.

Finally, peak hour auto travel time in minutes from the development's location (town) to Boston's central business district (CBD) is used to capture spatial quasi rents.

Regression Results

Regression estimates utilizing the three factors are summarized in Table 5-2. The equations reported here are all linear in the dependent variables. All the variables in Equation 5.3 are linear, and all have the expected relationship. The security factor is statistically significant under the one- and two-tailed tests, its coefficient being almost five times its standard error. The magnitude of the coefficient indicates that the multifamily housing market values this composite representation of tenant protection attributes very highly; a unit increase in this variable adds $120 to the rent (bundle price). Since the mean value of the dependent variable is $259.92, the security factor accounts for a substantial proportion of the rent. The adult recreation factor is statistically significant under a one-tailed test, which is appropriate because of strong a priori reasons to expect a positive sign on the variable. (Most of the variables analyzed in this section are accompanied with a strong expectation as to the direction of their effects.) The

Table 5-2

Coefficients of Regressions Relating Bundle Prices (Monthly Rent) to Various Attributes, Boston Metropolitan Area, 1972-73[a]

Variable	All Variables are Linear in Form		Travel Times and Median Income are Entered in Nonlinear Form	
	5.3	5.4	5.5	5.6
Factor 1 (Adult Recreation)	24.56 (1.72)	23.56 (1.55)	24.67 (1.72)	24.16 (1.59)
Factor 2 (Security)	120.0 (4.85)	117.4 (4.12)	119.6 (4.75)	117.0 (4.07)
Factor 3 (Family Services)	9.17 (0.65)	9.28 (0.55)	9.02 (0.64)	9.33 (0.56)
Excellent View	39.02 (3.70)	38.85 (2.93)	37.94 (3.60)	37.73 (2.87)
Yucky View	−14.17 (−1.55)	−17.06 (−1.57)	−14.21 (−1.54)	−17.83 (−1.64)
Median Income	0.0024 (1.24)	0.0026 (1.09)	−76.86 (−1.33)	−74.17 (−1.09)
Town-House Apartment	14.75 (1.54)	12.83 (1.18)	15.05 (1.57)	12.95 (1.20)
Utilities	15.14 (1.97)	17.48 (2.01)	14.82 (1.92)	17.56 (2.03)
Travel Time to CBD	−0.594 (−2.75)	−	98.09 (2.67)	−
Sectorized Travel Times to CBD				
North Shore	−	−0.591 (−1.93)	−	102.5 (2.08)
I-93	−	−0.531 (−1.79)	−	92.70 (1.96)
Route 2	−	−0.759 (−1.92)	−	123.9 (2.10)
Massachusetts Turnpike	−	−0.658 (−2.68)	−	110.8 (2.70)
Southwest Expressway	−	−0.591 (−2.19)	−	102.6 (2.29)
Southeast Expressway	−	−0.678 (−2.42)	−	121.7 (2.58)
Central Parts of Boston	−	−1.33 (−0.27)	−	286.0 (0.53)
Constant	235.8 (10.77)	236.5 (9.29)	198.5 (7.98)	−639.7 (−0.98)
R^2 (Corrected)	0.674	0.646	0.672	0.647
Degrees of Freedom	66	60	66	60
$t_{0.05}$ for one-tailed test	1.66	1.67	1.66	1.67

[a]The numbers in parentheses are the calculated t-statistics for the hypothesis that the coefficient is zero.

results indicate that a unit increase in this factor would add $24.56 to the rent, a significant proportion of the rent compared to its mean value in the sample. The third factor (family services) is not statistically significant and has a small coefficient compared to other terms in the equation; it appears that the market does not value facilities designed for families with children, which is consistent with the stereotyped view of demand for rental housing (young single persons or young married couples with no children).

The dummy variable on structure type shows that town-house apartments rent on the average for an additional $14.75 per month but the coefficient is not statistically significant at the two-tail 5 percent level. (A two-tailed test is more appropriate for this variable because there is no a priori view as to the market's valuation of different structure types.) Although there are two additional structure types (garden style and high-rise apartments), an additional dummy is not included because of the close relation to the presence of an elevator which is incorporated in the protection factor.

The dummy variable for utilities is included to correct for different pricing policies and performs as expected being significant at the one-tailed 5 percent level. The additional $15.14 per month included in rent for utilities is a reasonable figure.

Three neighborhood attributes or proxy variables are included in Equation 5.3. The excellent view variable is highly significant and indicates that a panoramic view of hills or water is worth $39.02 more than a pleasant view. Selecting a picturesque site for an apartment complex can give a developer a decided edge in the market place. A "yucky" view would tend to reduce rents by $14.17, but the coefficient is only statistically different than zero at the 7 percent level for a one-tail test. The census tract measure of neighborhood attributes does not perform as well as had been hoped; it does, however, work much better than using census descriptors of the town in which the development is located. Although the coefficient is not statistically significant at the 5 percent level, it has the expected relationship and indicates that a $1000 increase in median income would add $2.40 to the monthly rent. Experimentation with town and census tract measures of median income suggests that the median income of the neighborhood, an area centered about the apartment's location and perhaps smaller than a census tract, would work well in this equation. Even the present census tract variable performs well in some alternative specifications of the equation (Table 5-3).

Travel time from the apartment to Boston's CBD is included to measure spatial quasi rents. Its coefficient in Equation 5.3 is highly significant (two-tailed test) and indicates that a ten-minute increase in travel time would produce a $5.94 rent decrease. The product of the coefficient and the variable is largest in magnitude at the center of the metropolitan area and negative throughout the region. Since this variable also measures the decline in the price of a standardized bundle of residential attributes with distance from the region's center, which most economic theories of residential location predict, it is not possible to separate quasi rents from the overall rent gradient. In order to examine quasi rents in this submarket, the travel time variable is sectorized. That is, the metropolitan area is divided into six sectors, each of which includes at least one major highway providing access to the center of the region; a seventh subregion consists of the central areas of the city of Boston. Each variable takes a value of zero for towns not located in its sector or subregion and the value of travel time to Boston's CBD for towns located in its sector. Equation 5.4 uses the sectorized travel time variables in place of a single travel time variable (Table 5-2). The magnitudes and signs of the remaining variables are virtually the same as in Equation 5.3, but the adult recreation factor is now statistically insignificant at the one-tail 5 percent level, and the already weak median income variable is weakened. The sectorized travel time variables all have the negative relationship that economic theories of residential location predict. All the coefficients except that for the central parts of Boston are statistically significant at the one-tail 5 percent level. The central parts of Boston variable has the largest negative coefficient but is not significantly different than zero; there are only a few observations in this zone. By sectorizing the travel time variable, it was hoped that differences in the coefficients' values between sectors would add information about quasi rents in this submarket. Quasi rents might exist because zoning regulations are more receptive to apartment construction in some sectors than in other sectors. However, the coefficients could vary because of different rent gradients along each sector due to the multicentered nature of workplaces. And these combined with offsetting quasi rents could mask any quasi rents that may exist. Although the coefficients vary from -0.531 to -0.759, statistical tests show these differences to be insignificant.[8] One reason for no variation would be no quasi rents in this submarket, which would not be too unusual since one of the characteristics defining the submarket requires units to have been recently constructed. Current or recent activity in the production of a bundle in each sector implies no negative quasi rents.

Since many of the variables in Equations 5.3 and 5.4 have values between zero and one, the equations are reestimated using nonlinear measures of travel times and median income. The new measures are exponential: in the case of travel times, e is raised to a negative power which is equal to the product of 0.01 and the travel time; in the case of median income, e is raised to a negative power equal to 0.0001 times median income. The new variables have a maximum value of 1 when the travel time or median income is zero, and decrease as travel time or income increase. As a result, the signs of the estimated coefficients of these variables should be the opposite of those on the same variables in Equations 5.3 and 5.4. The new versions of the models are summarized in Table 5-2. Equations 5.5 and 5.6 are virtually identical to Equations 5.3 and 5.4, respectively. Each of the new sectorized travel time variables in Equation 5.6 increases the terms' significance. However, statistical tests comparing one sectorized travel time's coefficient to another produce the same results encountered in Equation 5.4: no evidence of quasi rents in this submarket. The only difference in the four equations is the size and significance of the intercept, which is much larger in magnitude in Equation 5.6 than in the other three, but negative and insignificantly different than zero. Each sectorized travel-time variable now has a value of one unless the observation is located in its sector. This is the reason for the substantial change in the intercept; in effect the old intercept (Equation 5.5) has been spread out among the seven zones and the new intercept. The fit of all four equations is quite good; two-thirds of the variance of the bundle prices (monthly rents), which ranges from $178 to $425, is explained. Overall fit does not provide a basis for choosing among the four equations. Equation 5.3 has also been estimated with the natural logarithm of bundle price as the dependent variable; the results closely parallel Equation 5.3 and the overall fit (R^2 of 0.648) is slightly lower.

Regression Results of Some Alternative Specifications

Several additional models are specified using individual attributes in place of the three factors (Table 5-3). Although the factors performed reasonably well, these other specifications should shed light on the relative importance of various individual attributes. Equation 5.7 is an individual specification model including each of the attributes that load heavily on one of the three factors and those variables which were entered individually in Equation 5.3. The four attributes contributing to the protection factor cumulatively add an average of $68.26 to the monthly rent; all four make positive contributions with security guards adding the largest single amount, almost half the total. Although none of these four variables is statistically significant at the 5 percent level (two-tailed test), there is enough multicollinearity in the data to make judgments on the basis of the t-statistics unwarranted. (Each of these four variables has a correlation of 0.4 or more with at least one other variable.) The coefficients, however, will be unbiased estimates if no relevant variables have been left out. Since the "true" relationship is not known, it is difficult, if not impossible, to say that this condition is satisfied.

Nine attributes contribute to the adult recreation factor. In Equation 5.7, their combined effect adds $21.14 to the monthly rent. However, four of them (exercise rooms, sauna, arts and crafts studio(s), and social director) show a negative relationship with bundle price; exercise rooms and sauna also have very small coefficients indicating they play virtually no role in distinguishing apartments within this submarket. The other two have rather large negative values ($13.45 for arts and crafts and $27.22 for social director); money spent on these attributes could have been better spent on some of the other attributes (security or tennis courts). Again these variables are statistically insignificant; arts and crafts and sauna have t-statistics which are nearly zero. Of the five

Table 5-3

Coefficients of Regressions Relating Bundle Prices (Monthly Rent) to Various Attributes, Boston Metropolitan Area, 1972-73[a]

Variable		All Variables are in Linear Form	
	5.7	5.8	5.9
Elevator	13.72	8.57	—
	(1.12)	(0.76)	
Covered Parking	16.49	11.17	—
	(1.17)	(0.87)	
Security Guards	27.95	26.68	—
	(1.61)	(1.67)	
Gatehouse for security	10.09	19.65	—
	(0.31)	(0.66)	
Exercise Rooms and Equipment	−0.261	−10.61	—
	(−0.01)	(−0.46)	
Sauna	−0.554	0.479	—
	(−0.03)	(0.03)	
Billiards	8.17	19.75	—
	(0.46)	(1.18)	
Shuffleboard	6.06	9.02	—
	(0.29)	(0.48)	
Handball or Squash	1.59	5.17	—
	(0.04)	(0.15)	
Function Room(s)	20.23	20.88	14.05
	(1.76)	(2.00)	(1.78)
Arts and Crafts Studio(s)	−13.45	−15.13	—
	(−0.64)	(−0.79)	
Woodworking Shop	26.57	32.23	—
	(0.55)	(0.74)	
Social Director	−27.22	−38.13	—
	(−1.15)	(−1.76)	
Basketball Court(s)	−10.36	−15.82	—
	(−0.91)	(−1.51)	
Tennis Court(s)	30.16	28.90	23.38
	(3.34)	(3.53)	(2.99)
Swimming Pool	−12.70	−15.63	—
	(−1.25)	(−1.60)	
Baseball Diamond(s)	3.84	−0.404	—
	(0.13)	(−0.02)	
Picnic Area	11.58	14.96	—
	(1.10)	(1.56)	
Playground	−21.31	−21.12	−25.79
	(−2.49)	(−2.71)	(−3.25)
Kindergarten, Daycare, or Babysitting Service	−22.82	−26.29	—
	(−1.06)	(−1.38)	
Dishwasher	—	18.36	—
		(1.92)	

Table 5-3 (cont.)

Variable	5.7	All Variables are in Linear Form 5.8	5.9
24-hour Maintenance	–	24.04 (2.59)	–
Laundry Facilities	–	27.01 (1.05)	–
Excellent View	38.21 (2.51)	31.41 (2.25)	49.71 (4.67)
Yucky View	−17.34 (−1.77)	−20.29 (−2.26)	−23.61 (−2.55)
Median Income	0.00505 (2.33)	0.0045 (2.26)	0.0061 (3.09)
Townhouse Apartment	12.49 (1.28)	13.39 (1.46)	–
Utilities	16.68 (1.95)	15.56 (2.00)	28.21 (3.90)
Travel Time to CBD	−0.813 (−3.34)	−0.880 (−3.96)	−1.23 (−6.70)
Constant	225.4 (9.09)	178.9 (5.58)	237.5 (10.32)
R^2 (Corrected)	0.695	0.749	0.635
Degrees of Freedom	49	46	67

[a]The numbers in parentheses are the calculated t-statistics for the hypothesis that the coefficient is zero.

attributes that have a positive relationship with bundle price, handball or squash facilities has a small coefficient; billiards and shuffleboard have moderate sized coefficients; and function room(s) and woodworking shop have relatively large coefficients (20.23 and 26.57, respectively). All five are also statistically insignificant.

The seven attributes composing the family services factor also show a dual pattern of behavior: five coefficients (basketball, swimming pool, playground and kindergarten) are negative, and three (tennis courts, baseball diamonds, and picnic area) are positive. One attribute in each sign category has a large coefficient and is statistically significant at the 5 percent level (two-tailed test)—playgrounds and tennis courts; the opposing pull of these two variables may be responsible for the rather poor performance of the family service factor in Equations 5.3 to 5.6. The strong negative relationship between playground and bundle price indicates that developments offering services aimed at children are devalued by the market; kindergarten's negative relationship supports while the picnic area and baseball diamond attributes' positive relationships detract from this hypothesis. The negative relationship between swimming pool and bundle price is surprising. It runs counter to the widespread view that pools are an important gathering place at developments catering to young single persons and young childless married couples; perhaps it is related to the high use of pools by mothers and their children.

The coefficients of the remaining six variables, except median income, demonstrate a high degree of stability across all five equations (5.3 to 5.7). The coefficient of the median income proxy for neighborhood attributes has doubled in magnitude and is now statistically significant at the 5 percent level (two-tailed test). In summary, five variables (excellent view, median income, travel time, playground and tennis courts) are statistically significant, at conventional levels, in Equation 5.7; many of the other variables may be statistically significant but multicollinearity precludes a test.

Attributes internal to the apartment and maintenance are not given weight in any of the preceding equations. For this reason dishwashers, laundry facilities, and twenty-four-hour maintenance service are added to Equation 5.7. The results are summarized in Equation 5.8 (Table 5-3). Most of the variables have similar coefficients; the only exceptions are exercise rooms (forty times larger), sauna (opposite sign), billiards (more than twice as large), handball (nearly three times as large) and baseball diamond (opposite sign and one-ninth its former magnitude). In addition, "yucky" view is statistically significant, and function room is nearly so. The new maintenance variable is statistically significant with a substantial positive coefficient ($24.04 per month) indicating that it is an important attribute not taken into account in the earlier formulations. The other new variables also have substantial coefficients but are not statistically significant, although dishwasher is nearly so. (None of the three new variables is highly correlated with any other variables; the highest simple correlation coefficient is 0.30.) The added variables slightly improve the corrected R^2.

If one were interested in a model to predict bundle prices at this point in time, a simpler version with fewer variables might be as accurate and, if so, should be favored over the more complex models. With this in mind, Equation 4.9 is estimated using function room, tennis courts, playground, excellent view, yucky view, median income, utilities, and travel time, which have been selected on the basis of their performance in Equations 5.7 and 5.8. The results are summarized in Equation 5.9 (Table 5-3). Adding twenty-four-hour maintenance and dishwashers does not appreciably improve the equation's fit, which is almost as good as all the equations fitted so far.[9] The standard error of the estimate in Equation 5.9 is 11 percent of the mean; the equations summarized in Table 5-2 and Equation 5.7 have standard errors of the estimate around 10 percent of the mean, and the figure for Equation 5.8 is just over 9 percent. If the relationship between any one of the included variables and the other attributes were to change, the use of this model to predict bundle prices at another time, or place, would be seriously compromised. For example, median income might not be as good a proxy for neighborhood attributes in the future or in a different metropolitan area.

A Simulation of Residential Choice

The preceding results provide the basis for simulating the residential choices of working households by making possible the prediction of the prices of a particular bundle at several different locations in the metropolitan area. For example, Equation 5.3 can be used to predict the price, or rent, of a particular bundle of attributes at different locations through variations in travel time to the CBD and neighborhood median income. In this section, this price surface is used to compare theoretically "best" residential locations with the actual locations selected by a group of households living in the new multifamily housing submarket. Before we proceed, the theory of residential location, sketched in Chapter 2, must be made more explicit.

Under the theory developed in Chapter 2, households select the location that minimizes the total costs of consuming the particular bundle they have chosen. These costs are referred to as *gross prices* and consist of the rent or price of the bundle plus all the household's transportation costs. Most of the *variation* in travel costs among alternative residential locations is attributable to journeys to and from work. Work trips account for over 40 percent of all trips.[10] For the most part, the remaining trips would be equally long and costly for all residential locations. Concentrating on the trips that provide the variation, work trips, greatly simplifies the analysis. (Note that this is *not* equivalent to assuming that there is only one workplace. The following simulation has as many possible workplaces as there are possible residential locations.) Work-trip costs have two parts: (a) the travel time involved (TC) and (b) the out-of-pocket travel costs ($OOPC$).

Therefore, the gross prices (GP) of a particular bundle are

$$GP(I,J,K) = RENT(J,K) + TC(I,J) + OOPC(I,J) \qquad 5.10$$

where $RENT(J,K)$ is the rent for bundle K at residence location J, and I is the household's workplace. $RENT(J,K)$ is obtained from the models in the preceding sections. To estimate time costs requires a fairly strong assumption, namely, that households place a monetary value on their travel time. In the present analysis, several values of travel time are tried; all involve some fraction of the wage rate. Out-of-pocket costs are estimated by assuming a peak hour travel speed of seventeen miles per hour and an average cost of eight cents per mile.

A sample of some 2800 households living in new multifamily housing in the Boston suburbs was gathered as part of this study. The sample was not drawn using statistical techniques such as random or area sampling. Instead, the sample was gathered seeking out the owners and/or managers of new suburban apartment developments willing to permit inspection of their tenant records; these are the forms filled out at the time current tenants applied for residence. The sample contains a description of each household's characteristics at the time of each household's decision to rent the apartment it occupied during the summer of 1972. Hence the data is uniquely suited for analyzing household residential location decisions. Fifteen developments in twelve different towns were covered; all the developments were conventionally financed. In addition to other information, the income and workplace of each household member was recorded.

Using the income and workplace of the head of each household in the sample, the travel costs between the workplace of each household and all possible residential locations can be calculated. The interzonal travel times are available for the 122 residential (workplace) zones of the Boston Air Quality Control Region (Figure 5-1). (The city of Boston is divided into eighteen zones; Cambridge, Newton, and Brookline are divided into two zones each; and the rest of the zones are cities and towns in the Boston metropolitan area.) The attributes of each household's housing bundle are also known and are utilized in Equations 5.3 to 5.9 to calculate a rent for this bundle in each of the 122 residence zones. Combining the two calculations gives an estimate of the gross price of this bundle in each of the 122 residence zones. The distribution of these 122 gross prices for each household ordered from lowest to highest is referred to as that household's *gross price distribution.*

According to the theory, each household should be living in the zone with the minimum gross price. If for each household the zones are ordered from the lowest to the highest gross price, the zone in which a household actually resides should be at or near the top. Since the models to be used to estimate the bundle rent are estimated for two-bedroom apartments in new multifamily housing, the simulation results for households occupying two-bedroom apartments are reported first. Five different values of travel time have been tried. Although the results reported here are simulated with Equation 5.9, all the equations produce similar distributions of gross prices. The results are summarized in Table 5-4, which divides the 122 positions in each household's gross price distribution into percentiles (groups of five positions). The table shows the percentage of households whose current residence location finished in each of these percentiles. For example, with a value of travel time equal to half the wage rate, the current residence zone of households in two-bedroom apartments is in the top 4.1 percent of the 122 possible positions (i.e., in the top five positions) in 29.1 percent of the cases. Forty-two point eight percent of these households choose a residential location (their current residence) for their preferred housing bundle such that it is within the lowest 12.3 percent of their gross price distributions. When travel time is given no value, the results are poor, but it is hard to distinguish among the results obtained with the four values of travel time greater than zero. Since the same pattern is present in the other simulations to be discussed, only the results for a value of travel time equal to half the wage rate are reported. The invariance in the distributions with different values of travel time implies that most of the differences in the ordering of alternative locations

Figure 5-1. Boston Air Quality Control Region.

is derived from the travel cost portion of the gross price. Such behavior would be reasonable in this submarket because only new housing is included, and the submarket is, therefore, likely to have small quasi rents. A simulation involving comparison of more types of rental housing bundles would probably show a marked improvement in explanatory power as the value of travel time

Table 5-4
The Percentage of Households Selecting a Residence Location for a Two-Bedroom Apartment in the Boston Outer Suburbs by its Place in Each Household's Gross Price Distribution, 1972

Percentile in Gross Price Distribution[a]	Equation 5.9 with Different Values of Travel Time				
	0.0	0.25	0.50	0.75	1.00
4.1	14.7	29.8	29.1	28.3	27.8
8.2	13.6	5.7	8.4	9.0	9.0
12.3	13.8	8.6	5.3	4.7	4.7
16.4	6.6	2.8	2.9	2.5	2.7
20.5	2.3	4.0	3.1	2.7	2.1
24.6	7.6	3.7	4.1	4.2	3.7
28.7	6.1	8.8	7.8	8.3	6.1
32.8	2.7	3.3	3.5	3.0	6.1
36.9	1.0	3.9	4.7	4.5	4.0
41.0	1.9	1.1	1.2	2.4	2.8
45.1	6.8	9.2	9.0	4.6	2.1
49.2	1.1	5.7	3.7	8.0	10.8
53.3	2.3	3.5	2.1	1.6	1.0
57.4	2.1	1.6	3.0	2.4	3.1
61.5	15.1	1.8	2.8	2.4	1.7
65.6	0.7	3.6	4.5	3.4	2.3
69.7	0.9	2.0	2.9	5.5	6.5
73.8	0.0	0.4	0.6	0.6	1.4
77.9	0.6	0.0	0.3	0.4	0.5
82.0	0.0	0.4	0.4	0.9	0.6
86.1	0.0	0.2	0.0	0.0	0.5
90.2	0.1	0.2	0.2	0.0	0.0
94.3	0.0	0.0	0.5	0.6	0.6
98.4	0.0	0.0	0.0	0.1	0.1
100.0	0.0	0.0	0.0	0.0	0.0
Number of Households	1011	1011	1011	1011	1011

[a]The percentile references the end point of the interval.

approached the wage rate. An analysis of the Pittsburgh rental housing market including bundle types descriptive of the whole rental stock, by John Quigley, found that a gross price formulation was consistently more powerful for larger values of travel time.[11]

The ranking of gross prices disaggregated by the head's workplace (Boston's

CBD, the rest of the city of Boston, and the suburban ring) is also investigated. The results are summarized in Table 5-5. It is evident that gross prices are excellent predictors of the residential location decisions of households with heads working in the suburbs; 65.4 percent of them choose a residence location in the lowest 12.3 percent of their gross price distribution. However, it performs poorly for CBD workers and only slightly better for other central city workers.[12] Failure to define the submarket in terms of neighborhood character-istics may be part of the reason. That is, there are probably zones whose gross prices, as calculated here, would be less than the current residence zone but whose neighborhoods are considered too dense, "rough," or undesirable in some way for the households in the sample to live in them; inclusion of neighborhood in the definition of the submarket would have eliminated these areas from consideration. The median income variable in Equations 5.3 to 5.9 captures the price variation but does not permit an adequate reflection of household preferences for neighborhoods; this is not surprising for it was not designed to do so. Roughly three-tenths of the zones with gross prices lower than that of the current residence zone of the CBD worker households are low-income or high-density zones in the city of Boston (six in the downtown area and others in South Boston, East Boston, Charlestown, Roxbury, and North Dorchester). If these zones were undesirable neighborhoods for some reason, more careful attention to neighborhood characteristics would probably improve the model's performance. For the suburban workers, some zones rank ahead of their current residence zone, due to the partial treatment of neighborhood.

Another reason for the poor performance of the model for centrally employed persons may be the lower density (sometimes as low as 12 units per acre), and larger amount of open space generally provided by the suburban developments but unavailable with the high-rise apartments constructed in the CBD or with the few garden style apartments (two to four story structures) found in other parts of the central city. Households with centrally employed workers that seek such amenities as open space, outdoor athletic facilities, and a country-like setting would only find them in the newer suburban apartment developments. The model would also be more accurate if the simulation were to take into consideration all the work trips made by the members of each household; that is, if multiple worker households were explicitly accounted for.

Finally, the model should perform better for suburban than for central city workers because the centrally employed worker has more alternatives that are reasonable to evaluate. He has more transportation modes to choose from and is closer to a larger variety of housing stock. For the same range of gross prices, the central city worker enjoys a larger assortment of housing types from which to make a choice than does the suburban worker. Since workers do not have complete information (prices, travel times, etc.) about their alternatives and since the central city worker has more relevant alternatives, central city workers' behavior is likely to show more variation in terms of this model than that of suburban workers.

Table 5-5

The Percentage of Households Selecting a Residence Location for a Two-Bedroom Apartment in the Boston Outer Suburbs by its Place in Each Household's Gross Price Distribution by Workplace, 1972

| Percentile in Gross Price Distribution[a] | Equation 5.9 with Travel Time Valued at 0.5 Times the Wage Rate | | |
	CBD Workers	Other Central City Workers	Suburban Ring Workers
4.1	0.0	0.0	46.0
8.2	0.0	0.0	13.3
12.3	0.0	16.3	6.1
16.4	0.0	0.0	4.5
20.5	0.0	1.1	4.7
24.6	0.0	9.9	5.0
28.7	19.6	10.9	2.2
32.8	1.4	17.4	3.0
36.9	7.1	5.4	3.6
41.0	0.7	5.4	0.8
45.1	26.1	6.5	2.0
49.2	9.3	1.1	1.6
53.3	0.4	6.5	2.2
57.4	5.0	0.0	2.5
61.5	6.8	2.2	1.1
65.6	12.5	5.4	0.9
69.7	9.6	1.1	0.2
73.8	0.0	4.3	0.2
77.9	1.1	0.0	0.0
82.0	0.4	2.2	0.2
86.1	0.0	0.0	0.0
90.2	0.0	2.2	0.0
94.3	0.0	2.2	0.5
98.4	0.0	0.0	0.0
100.0	0.0	0.0	0.0
Number of Households	280	92	639

[a]The percentile references the end point of the interval.

The coefficients of the median income and travel time variables in Equations 5.3 to 5.9 produce the distributions of gross prices. If it is assumed that these coefficients will be similar in the cases of one- and three-bedroom apartments, the simulation can be extended to these units. Tables 5-6 and 5-7 present the results of such simulations. Again the model simulates the behavior of suburban

Table 5-6
The Percentage of Households Selecting a Residence Location for a One-Bedroom Apartment in the Boston Outer Suburbs by its Place in Each Household's Gross Price Distribution by Workplace, 1972

Percentile in Gross Price Distribution[a]	Equation 5.9 with Travel Time Valued at 0.5 Times the Wage Rate		
	CBD Workers	Other Central City Workers	Suburban Ring Workers
4.1	0.0	0.0	46.7
8.2	0.0	0.0	12.6
12.3	0.0	22.1	8.0
16.4	0.0	0.0	5.2
20.5	0.0	1.3	3.0
24.6	0.0	19.5	4.1
28.7	21.1	14.3	1.9
32.8	5.0	22.1	3.3
36.9	16.1	2.6	2.6
41.0	1.0	1.3	1.3
45.1	35.7	2.6	1.7
49.2	4.5	3.9	2.4
53.3	1.0	5.2	2.0
57.4	2.0	1.3	0.7
61.5	5.0	1.3	1.5
65.6	4.0	0.0	0.2
69.7	3.0	0.0	1.1
73.8	0.5	1.3	0.2
77.9	1.0	1.3	0.2
82.0	0.0	0.0	0.0
86.1	0.0	0.0	0.7
90.2	0.0	0.0	0.6
94.3	0.0	0.0	0.0
98.4	0.0	0.0	0.0
100.0	0.0	0.0	0.0
Number of Households	199	77	538

[a]The percentile references the end point of the interval.

workers more accurately than that of CBD or other central city workers: 67.3 percent of the households demanding one-bedroom apartments and 61.2 percent of those demanding three-bedroom apartments choose a residence location in the lowest 12.3 percent of the gross price distribution. In general, two-thirds of the households working in the suburban ring are making residential location

Table 5-7

The Percentage of Households Selecting a Residence Location for a Three-Bedroom Apartment in the Boston Outer Suburbs by its Place in Each Household's Gross Price Distribution by Workplace, 1972

Percentile in Gross Price Distribution[a]	Equation 5.9 with Travel Time Valued at 0.5 Times the Wage Rate		
	CBD Workers	Other Central City Workers	Suburban Ring Workers
4.1	0.0	0.0	40.3
8.2	0.0	0.0	5.6
12.3	0.0	18.9	15.3
16.4	0.0	0.0	7.6
20.5	0.0	0.0	2.8
24.6	0.0	16.2	9.0
28.7	58.2	5.4	2.1
32.8	5.5	21.6	2.8
36.9	0.0	8.1	1.4
41.0	0.0	16.2	2.1
45.1	11.0	2.7	2.1
49.2	12.1	2.7	2.1
53.3	0.0	0.0	1.4
57.4	0.0	0.0	2.8
61.5	0.0	2.7	0.7
65.6	6.6	0.0	0.0
69.7	6.6	5.4	1.4
73.8	0.0	0.0	0.0
77.9	0.0	0.0	0.0
82.0	0.0	0.0	0.0
86.1	0.0	0.0	0.0
90.2	0.0	0.0	0.0
94.3	0.0	0.0	0.7
98.4	0.0	0.0	0.0
100.0	0.0	0.0	0.0
Number of Households	91	37	144

[a]The percentile references the end point of the interval.

decisions consistent with this theory of residential location. Considering the simplified version employed here (e.g., no specific account of multiple worker households and inadequate treatment of neighborhood characteristics), this is a high measure of accuracy and strong support for the theory.

Summary

The heterogeneity of the housing stock and the spatial distribution of employment sites have hampered the analysis of intrametropolitan household residential location decisions. In this chapter, the heterogeneity of housing is recognized by examining the attributes that are provided by dwelling units and their locations. And disequilibrium in the context of a durable good with a spatial distribution is introduced in the form of spatial quasi rents. Together these concepts set the stage for analyzing the multifamily housing market by developing hedonic price indexes. Such indexes are calculated for a sample of new two-bedroom apartments in the Boston metropolitan area and are used to identify the more important attributes and to examine their market values. A factor analysis with thirty-two attributes of these apartments indicates three composite measures of services demanded by households: adult recreation facilities, personal security, and outdoor recreation facilities that are likely to interest families with children. These three factors account for over half the mean monthly rent when used as variables in a hedonic price index. Only the adult recreation and security variables, however, are statistically significant. When the three composite variables are replaced by the attributes that load heavily on them, the four implicit prices associated with security (gatehouse, security guards, covered parking, and elevators) all are positive and sizeable. The implicit prices on the attributes composing the other composite variables have mixed signs and magnitudes. In general, security, tennis courts, and function rooms are highly valued, and playgrounds, swimming pools, and social directors are unwanted (sizeable negative implicit prices).

The hedonic price indexes also indicate that consumers are willing to pay more for a town-house style apartment, a large sum for an apartment with a panoramic view of hills or water, and a small sum for apartments in higher income neighborhoods. Sizeable spatial quasi rents do not beset this submarket which is to be expected because of current production activity in the submarket.

The implicit prices from the hedonic price indexes are used to simulate the residential location decisions of households now living in suburban apartments. The simulation allows each household to view its particular bundle of housing attributes at all 122 possible residential locations from its workplace. The results provide support for the theory that households select the residential location that minimizes their total location costs or their gross price of housing (house price or rent plus commuting costs); 43 percent of the households choose a residential location in the lowest 12.3 percent of their gross price distributions. The percentage is even higher for households with jobs in the suburbs—65 percent.

6

Suburban Apartments and Restrictive Zoning Ordinances

Suburban zoning laws are coming under heavy attack as devices that have the effect of excluding the poor from suburban neighborhoods. Much of this debate is premised on the assumption that laws, which on their face prohibit an activity, are the reason or cause that the activity does not occur. This assumption emphasizes the supply side of the housing market to the exclusion of the demand side. Although laws are passed to achieve specific objectives, there are several ways that a law which does not alter behavior patterns might be enacted. For example, laws are generally passed with a multitude of objectives in mind and, as a result, only some of these objectives may be served. Laws may also be failures and frequently have unintended effects that are unrelated to their objectives. Often, too, the benefits and costs of each piece of legislation are merely *perceived* by the proponents and opponents; that is, unrealistic fears or ignorance may lead to the passage of ineffective laws. Before one can say that any particular law alters behavior patterns (that is, is binding), it is necessary to know what behavior would have occurred in the absence of that law. This chapter examines this question for local zoning regulations that have the apparent effect of restricting apartment construction.

Zoning laws, in general, are enacted by local governments (cities, towns, villages, and counties) under authority delegated to them by state governments. These laws regulate land use within the borders of each jurisdiction by describing the types of buildings and the lot sizes which will be allowed in each part of the community. Their general purpose is to prevent construction on any site which would detract unreasonably from the use of neighboring property.

Suburban zoning ordinances have been attacked for excluding mobile homes, apartments, and other categories of residential land use.[1] In addition, suburban ordinances that restrict single-family housing to three-acre lots have been attacked by builders who want to construct similar housing on one-acre lots.[2] The opinions in these cases do not have a guiding principle, and they often result in a narrow supply-side evaluation of the facts. In our examination of zoning ordinances that prohibit apartment construction in a community, the basic issue is whether such an ordinance has had an effect on land use in that community. If there were no prohibition, would apartments be in demand in the community? This is an empirical question; economic theory does not provide a unique answer. Zoning laws may be binding in only some towns, in all towns, or in no towns. If zoning laws that restrict apartment construction are not binding, then organizations that are attacking these laws to open the suburbs to low-income families (for example, Suburban Action Inc. in the New York metropolitan area) are wasting their resources. Successful attacks on nonbinding zoning ordinances will not alter the pattern of residential land use in the metropolitan area.

A theory of residential location decision making by households is needed to predict socioeconomic behavior in the absence of zoning laws. Fortunately, urban economics has developed enough to provide a framework that is useful for analyzing and simulating residential location decisions.[3] According to this theory, households with at least one wage earner select a residence location for their preferred bundle of housing attributes (number of bedrooms, yard space, interior design, etc.) that minimizes their total costs of residential location. The total costs are the cost of the housing (rent or purchase price) *plus* the cost of travel (out-of-pocket costs and value of time spent traveling) by household members. Since the price of any given bundle of housing attributes exhibits intrametropolitan spatial variations, a household that desires a relatively large bundle of housing attributes may find that it can generate net savings by incurring a longer journey to work. In fact, the price of any given quantity of housing generally declines with distance from the household head's place of work. Therefore households will incur added travel costs (a longer journey to work) to obtain lower housing prices until the marginal savings in housing price is equal to the marginal costs of a longer work trip.

In Chapter 5, we constructed a simulation model of the residential location choices of suburban apartment residents on the basis of this theory. The price of an apartment that contains a certain bundle of housing attributes was estimated, with an hedonic price index, for all locations within the Boston metropolitan area. The actual residential location decisions of the 2800 suburban apartment residents that were studied in Chapter 5 can be compared with the simulated choices to shed light on the question of whether local zoning ordinances are altering behavioral decisions. That is, the simulation will represent a household's choice without zoning regulations, and the actual choice will be subject to the zoning laws then in existence. If the locations that are selected in the simulation are (a) different than those actually selected and (b) subject to zoning regulations that prevent apartment construction, it is fair to imply that zoning ordinances in these towns are binding.

Zoning Restrictions

All the cities and towns in the Air Quality Control Region, the geographic area covered by the simulation (Chapter 5), that have restrictive zoning ordinances or that had a low 1960-70 productivity of multifamily housing (less than seventy-six new units of housing in buildings with five or more dwelling units) were identified. During each simulation, a record was kept of the number of times that each of these towns had a gross price in an individual's gross price distribution below the gross price corresponding to that household's current residence location. The results by bedroom and workplace are presented in Table 6-1. along with the median family income (1969) and zoning policy of each town. The towns in Table 6-1 are organized into four categories of 1960-70 housing production on the basis of the *1970 Census of Housing*: (a) no construction of buildings with five or more dwelling units (twenty-four towns); (b) construction of some such buildings but less than fifty units (thirteen towns); (c) construction of such buildings for a town total of at least fifty units, but no more than seventy-five units (eleven towns), and (d) other towns that have restrictive zoning practices but have had more than seventy-five units of multifamily housing constructed between 1960 and 1970 (sixteen towns). These towns are located in Boston's outer suburbs; nearly all are over forty minutes from downtown Boston during rush hour traffic conditions. Forty-two of the sixty-four towns have median family incomes above $11,448, the median family income for the Boston standard metropolitan statistical area in 1970. Sixteen of the seventeen towns in the Boston Air Quality Control Region that have median family incomes above $14,000 are among the towns in Table 6-1.

Since the simulation is most effective for suburban workers, most credence should be given to their results. However, Table 6-1 must be read carefully; the same household can contribute to the town specific counts of more than one town. For example, if both Dover and Pembroke had gross prices less than the gross price of a household's actual residence zone, the count for each town would be increased by one. Therefore the reader should avoid interpreting the figures in Table 6-1 as simultaneous demand in the various towns. They are, however, indicative of the demand for multifamily housing units. Towns that have a simulated demand in excess of supply are referred to as having unmet demands for multifamily housing. When each town's simulated demand for multifamily housing is compared to its zoning policy, we can make a coarse estimate of the effect of the various zoning policies on household residential location decisions.

Although information on zoning laws is available for most of the sixty-four cities and towns in Table 6-1, it is not free of ambiguity in every case.[4] According to the information available, Acton, Bolton, Boxborough, Cohasset, Dover, Duxbury, Essex, Hanover, Holliston, Lynnfield, Marshfield, Nahant, Norfolk, Norwell, Sherborn, Southborough, Stow, Sudbury, Topsfield, Wayland, and Wenham do not allow apartments. (Lynnfield and Nahant were combined into one zone for the simulation.) In addition, Bedford, Milton, and Wilmington only allow apartments that are constructed for the elderly with government assistance. Some additional towns that apparently allow apartment construction but only at very low densities (units per acre in parentheses) are: Ashland (5.5), Braintree (22.0), Dedham (5.9), Foxborough (23.5), Lexington (18.0), Lincoln (5.5), Millis (7.3), Natick (14.7), Norwood (17.6), Saugus (17.6), Sharon (8.8), Stoughton (5.5), Walpole (12.6), Wellesley (24.4), Weston (4.4), Westwood

Table 6-1
Selected Characteristics of the Supply-Constrained Towns in 1970 and the Number of Times a Supply-Constrained Town had a Gross Price below the Gross Price for the Location Actually Selected by Workplace, Apartment Size, and Degree of Supply Constraint, 1972

	Zoning Practice[a]	Median Family Income	One-Bedroom Units			Two-Bedroom Units			Three-Bedroom Units		
			CBD Workplace	Other CC Workplace	Suburban Workplace	CBD Workplace	Other CC Workplace	Suburban Workplace	CBD Workplace	Other CC Workplace	Suburban Workplace
						No New Apartments 1960-1970					
Avon	NI	$11,638	31	11	57	100	31	45	12	8	12
Bolton	R	11,098	1	1	75	1	5	68	0	0	14
Cohasset	R	13,622	3	3	18	8	18	17	3	4	9
Dover	R	21,460	0	1	15	0	3	13	0	1	1
Duxbury	R	12,938	0	1	6	0	10	8	0	1	7
Hanover	R	12,831	18	3	16	77	18	20	12	4	8
Hingham	A	13,189	25	4	20	85	20	23	12	4	10
Hopkinton	NI	10,732	2	3	79	1	7	61	0	0	15
Hull	A	9,766	36	7	22	97	20	23	10	5	10
Lynnfield and Nahant	R	15,199	14	6	35	56	8	56	12	4	14
Norfolk	R	11,307	1	5	60	1	12	49	0	3	20
Norwell	R	13,449	25	4	15	86	23	18	12	7	9
Pembroke	AR	10,795	12	3	17	27	17	20	1	3	7
Sherborn	R	16,855	0	1	31	0	5	27	0	0	14
Southborough	R	12,434	0	3	82	1	7	63	0	0	17

Stow	R	12,202	0	1	83	0	6	82	0	0	15
Sudbury	R	17,273	0	1	52	0	6	51	0	0	14
Topsfield	R	15,912	0	1	8	0	1	12	0	0	6
Wayland	R	16,675	0	1	94	10	10	109	3	1	22
Wenham	R	13,044	0	4	16	0	2	24	0	0	6
W. Bridgewater	NI	10,788	8	5	48	10	18	40	0	3	9
Whitman	NI	10,166	35	6	33	101	20	33	12	5	8
Wilmington	RE	11,317	112	7	64	197	20	98	33	2	22
Less than Fifty Units of New Apartments 1960-1970											
Bedford	RE	13,671	2	1	117	4	6	127	0	0	31
Boxborough	R	12,147	0	1	79	0	6	86	0	0	11
Bridgewater	NI	10,020	4	3	15	3	17	18	0	2	7
E. Bridgewater	NI	10,313	9	4	32	14	17	33	0	3	7
Hamilton	A	11,633	0	4	24	1	4	40	0	0	7
Hanson	NI	10,878	7	3	18	9	16	22	0	3	7
Maynard	AR	9,692	41	14	147	110	21	155	12	3	25
Medfield	A	14,611	0	5	50	1	13	38	0	3	20
Milton	RE	13,605	129	40	38	45	216	64	38	25	21
Sharon	DR	14,391	0	3	38	0	13	29	0	2	12
Swampscott	A	12,312	110	12	22	197	26	56	33	5	12
Weston	DR	22,136	0	1	20	1	5	40	1	0	6
Westwood	DR	16,153	0	5	37	7	21	30	2	5	10

(continued)

Table 6-1 (cont.)

	Zoning Practice[a]	Median Family Income	One-Bedroom Units			Two-Bedroom Units			Three-Bedroom Units		
			CBD Workplace	Other CC Workplace	Suburban Workplace	CBD Workplace	Other CC Workplace	Suburban Workplace	CBD Workplace	Other CC Workplace	Suburban Workplace
Fifty to Seventy-five New Apartments 1960-1970											
Abington	NI	$10,523	113	11	38	199	35	39	33	11	12
Concord	A	14,640	4	1	100	16	6	110	5	0	21
Essex	R	9,442	4	4	27	2	5	46	0	0	6
Hudson	A	10,570	2	2	117	1	7	113	0	0	21
Marshfield	R	11,417	0	1	12	1	11	9	0	0	7
Middleton	A	10,620	20	6	47	37	15	71	4	0	13
Millis	DR	11,898	2	7	69	4	16	53	0	4	21
North Reading	AR	12,173	15	6	46	60	8	62	11	0	13
Rockland	A	9,999	129	26	40	209	50	38	33	19	12
Scituate	A	12,441	0	2	18	3	15	13	0	3	8
Wellesley	DR	16,879	15	4	78	74	22	83	14	5	20
Towns with Restrictive Zoning and More than Seventy-five New Apartments 1960-1970											
Acton	R	$14,402	0	1	78	0	5	78	0	0	13
Ashland	DR	11,468	0	3	93	1	6	73	0	0	18
Braintree	DR	12,330	136	32	54	201	46	40	33	22	15
Danvers	AR	11,730	26	7	46	77	13	76	12	2	15
Dedham	DR	11,691	116	53	138	187	70	128	33	31	33
Foxborough	DR	11,243	1	3	43	1	8	34	0	0	10

Holliston	R	12,527	0	3	43	0	7	38	0	0	16
Lexington	DR	16,160	14	1	86	51	12	103	12	3	20
Lincoln	DR	16,687	4	1	87	20	9	89	5	0	15
Marblehead	AR	12,718	26	8	15	81	13	42	12	4	8
Natick	DR	12,104	30	9	119	90	22	133	12	6	28
Norwood	DR	11,474	32	22	50	96	36	43	12	15	11
Saugus	DR	10,974	157	13	57	204	25	84	33	5	15
Stoughton	DR	11,151	33	9	59	92	20	44	12	6	14
Walpole	DR	12,259	3	8	47	3	21	40	0	6	15
Winchester	DR	14,817	53	7	73	147	20	95	28	5	21

[a]The zoning code is:

  R Apartments are excluded.
  RE Apartments are excluded except for government assisted housing for the elderly.
  DR Low-density restriction.
  AR Ambiguous restriction.
  A Apartments are allowed.
  NI No information.

(11.0), and Winchester (11.7). The towns of Danvers, Marblehead, Maynard, North Reading, and Pembroke have some rather ambiguous zoning requirements that may restrict apartment development. The towns of Concord, Hamilton, Hingham, Hudson, Hull, Medfield, Middleton, Rockland, Scituate, and Swampscott allow apartment development. Zoning information was unavailable for Abington, Avon, Bridgewater, East Bridgewater, Hanson, Hopkinton, West Bridgewater, and Whitman.

The results of the simulation are summarized in Table 6-2. Nine of the twenty-three towns that exclude apartments show no unmet demand for apartments while only three towns exhibit unmet demand. The remaining eleven towns that exclude apartments divide almost evenly between towns that probably have no unmet demand and towns that probably have some unmet demand. The twenty-two towns that have other types of restrictive zoning practices exhibit more unmet demand but still have four towns that exhibit none and another three that probably have none. The ten towns without restrictive zoning laws include towns with and without unmet demands. If the zoning regulations are binding constraints that alter residential location decisions in the housing market, we would expect towns that have restrictive zoning ordinances to exhibit an unmet demand for apartments. Although some of these towns (Bedford, Braintree, Dedham, Lexington, Maynard, Milton, Natick, Norwood, Saugus, Wellesley, Wilmington, and Winchester) exhibit unmet demands for apartments, many of them do not (Cohasset, Dover, Duxbury, Essex, Foxborough, Holliston, Marshfield, Pembroke, Sharon, Sherborn, Topsfield, Wen-

Table 6-2
Predicted Level of Free Market Demand by Type of Zoning Ordinance for Sixty-three Towns in the Boston AQCR: 1972

Type of Zoning Ordinance	Predicted Level of Free Market Demand			
	No Unmet Demand	Probably No Unmet Demand	Probably Some Unmet Demand	Unmet Demand
Zoning Ordinances Do Not Allow Apartments	9	6	5	3
Other Types of Restrictive Zoning Ordinances (Largely Low-Density Requirements)	4	3	6	9
No Restrictive Zoning Ordinances	2	1	5	2
No Zoning Information	2	3	1	2
Totals	17	13	18	15

ham, and Weston). The null hypothesis that the towns are equally distributed between unmet and no unmet demand regardless of zoning laws was tested with the chi-square measure. Unmet demand and probably some unmet demand were combined, and no unmet demand and probably no unmet demand were combined, for the test to reduce the discontinuity error arising from the small sample size. The two categories of restrictive zoning were also combined, and the towns without zoning information were excluded. The chi-square test statistic is 1.13. For the one degree of freedom in our 2 x 2 table a chi square of 3.84 or larger is required to reject the null hypothesis at the 5 percent level of significance. Since our chi-square test statistic is less than 3.84, we cannot reject the null hypothesis that the patterns of unmet demand do not differ with respect to the type of zoning law.

Discussions with real estate development firms active in the suburban apartment market indicate that the availability of sewer and water facilities is also an important constraint on their decisions concerning site selection and acquisition. A 1965 inventory of sewer facilities categorized the following cities and towns in the area containing our 122 zones as having no public sewer facilities: Acton, Ashland, Avon, Boxborough, Burlington, Cohasset, Dover, Duxbury, East Bridgewater, Easton, Essex, Hamilton, Hanover, Hanson, Holbrook, Holliston, Hopkinton, Lincoln, Lynnfield, Middleton, Norfolk, North Reading, Norwell, Pembroke, Rockland, Scituate, Sharon, Sherborn, Southborough, Stow, Sudbury, Topsfield, Wayland, Wenham, West Bridgewater, Weston, and Whitman.[5] Boxborough, Sherborn, and Stow also did not have public water supplies in 1965.[6] A comparison of these towns with those having unmet demands produces the same mixed results as in the case of zoning regulations. Although there is a good deal of overlap between towns with restrictive zoning ordinances and those without public sewer facilities, Middleton, a town showing unmet demand, is classified as allowing apartments but not having public sewers. At the same time, Burlington has had substantial apartment development without public sewers. Cohasset, Dover, Duxbury, Essex, Holliston, Pembroke, Sharon, Sherborn, Topsfield, Wenham, and Weston have both restrictive zoning regulations and no public sewer facilities, but show no unmet demand for apartments. In addition, there are towns—Acton, Ashland, and Lincoln for example—that have both constraints on apartment development, but have allowed more than 120 units of multifamily housing to be constructed during the last decade. In fact, 569 units were constructed in Acton during this period. Finally, Concord, Hudson, Maynard, and Wilmington have neither restriction but have unmet demands for apartments.

Summary

Although restrictive zoning regulations and lack of public sewer service do not have a cut and dried effect on apartment development, they do seem to retard its progress. At the same time, it is important to realize that restrictive zoning ordinances and/or lack of public sewer facilities do not prevent apartment development in many towns, which because of their locations, are not currently in demand by apartment dwellers. Sixteen of the forty-five towns that have restrictive zoning practices contain more than seventy-five units of multifamily housing that were constructed in the last decade. Five of these sixteen exhibit unmet demand. Seventeen of the twenty-nine towns that have restrictive zoning ordinances and that contain less than seventy-five units of new multifamily housing are not in demand as residential locations by apartment dwellers. However, twelve of these twenty-nine towns are in demand.

Since zoning regulations are not always binding, organizations that are attacking zoning provisions face a difficult task in identifying communities that have restrictive zoning provisions which are also binding. If their efforts lead to a judicial decision declaring illegal a zoning law that does not alter behavior, they will not have had much, if any, impact on the allocation of residential land within that metropolitan area. Any benefit would flow from that decision as a precedent for later cases against communities that have restrictive and binding zoning regulations. These organizations would best serve their purposes by selecting such communities at the start. And one suspects that a stronger case could be presented against a zoning regulation for excluding some land use and indirectly low-income families when that regulation actually has that effect.

Litigation over zoning laws usually involves either general and ambiguous state legislation that delegates the zoning power to local governments or the ill-defined constitutional limitation that requires the ordinance to be in reasonable furtherance of the public health, safety, morals, or general welfare. Although recent judicial decisions show an increased sensitivity to the regional consequences of local housing policy, a consistent set of standards that are adequate to assess zoning laws have not evolved.[7] Courts find themselves venturing into housing market analysis; one recent case made a finding that "there would be no market" for the high rental apartments that the zoning ordinance sanctioned.[8] The evaluation of the impacts of a zoning ordinance, then, is no simple matter; an ordinance that appears on its face to be very restrictive may only prove to be a reflection of the land-use pattern that would have emerged in an unregulated housing market. Our inadequate understanding of the socioeconomic aspects of land-use decisions and the impact of land-use controls has been a major inhibitor of the development of judicial standards for evaluating zoning laws. State legislatures should provide the courts and the local governments with more guidance and should sponsor socioeconomic research aimed at delineating reliable standards.

7 The Future of Apartments in the Central City

Edgar Hoover and Raymond Vernon, in their classic study of the New York metropolitan region in the late 1950s, characterize the demand for residences, largely apartments, in the central areas of the region (Manhattan) as coming from the "very rich and the very poor."[1] The poor (low-income unskilled manual and service workers and members of minority groups)

are there because of the supply of obsolete, dilapidated, and highly compressed housing; because their jobs are mainly in Manhattan and nearby heavy industry zones, and the subway affords cheap access; because they are excluded from most . . . suburbs by social counter-pressures as well as by lack of rock-bottom housing; and because they find some community solidarity and better job opportunity within the focal cluster and its huge and variegated labor market. The other conspicuous element in the inner Core (far smaller, and mainly confined to certain sections of Manhattan) consists of wealthy and mainly childless people in the professional and executive categories, who value quick access to their Manhattan jobs and also the many vocational attractions of the region's center, and who have been able to afford the high costs of luxury-apartment redevelopment.[2]

Hoover and Vernon also conclude that centrally employed, high-income families not living in the core lived in single-family homes on ample lots (8000 square feet and up) in older zoning protected suburbs (e.g., Scarsdale), in new suburbs (e.g., Somerset and Bergen counties in New Jersey), or in "exurbia" (e.g., Orange and Dutchess counties and the northern portion of Westchester County in New York). They believe that the presence or absence of children is the most important single factor influencing the choice between centrally located apartments and suburban single-family homes, and that higher income families have a high propensity to choose a low-density community as soon as children appear.

As part of the upsurge of apartment construction in the 1960s, a large number of high-rent apartments have been constructed in or near the central business districts of cities all across the country, sometimes on land cleared with urban renewal funds. In fact, one of the goals of the urban renewal program has been to attract higher income families to the central city as a place of residence.[3] This construction activity in the central-city luxury apartment market has formed the basis, in part, of optimistic predictions about the future of central cities. Whether central cities have retained, or increased, their share of childless, high-income families is crucial to the interpretation of the recent construction activity and bears on the central city's future. The suburbanization

101

of apartments raises the question of whether childless, high-income families have continued to be as important a force in the demand for central city luxury apartments as in the past.

During April 1970, the Boston Redevelopment Authority (BRA) mailed a questionnaire to the 2181 apartments in two new high-rise apartment complexes in Boston's central business district (Charles River Park and the Prudential Apartments), and received 632 responses.[4] By comparing the respondents' characteristics to those of the population of the city of Boston as described in the *1970 Census of Population*, the BRA arrived at the following "vision of the future of Boston":

The new residential tower occupants have higher income levels. A much larger portion had not lived in Boston before. They had a greater concentration of 1 and 2 person households, and they were older. The rentals they paid were considerably higher.[5]

The results of the comparison are in general no surprise. Since the surveyed apartments are new, unsubsidized, and of high-rise construction, the rents and consequently the occupants' incomes should exceed Boston's rents and the incomes of Boston residents as a whole. That the households in the apartments are smaller than the city's households is explained by factors affecting the choice of structure type and no more. The BRA interprets the higher incomes and the large fraction of apartment dwellers who had moved from outside the city as a return of middle- and upper-income people to the central city. Most of those coming from outside the city of Boston are in-migrants to the SMSA, and it is not surprising that they should select an apartment during their initial period of adjustment to a new area. As to the remainder, the report makes no systematic inquiry into the reasons for choosing apartments and for selecting the central city. Such an approach might provide some basis for the BRA's projection.

If the BRA had conducted a survey of the occupants of the new housing built under the federal government's subsidized housing programs, the vision of the future Boston would have been quite different. The incomes would have been lower and the families larger. The BRA selected the group that personified its vision of Boston and projected that group's characteristics as those of the future Boston. To justify a set of characteristics as a picture of the future requires some comparison, over time, of the city's composition that indicates movement toward that set of characteristics. For example, if the future Boston population is to be projected to have higher incomes, that projection should be based on an increase in the real incomes of Boston residents as a whole, on a shift in the overall distribution of their incomes over time after accounting for increases in real income, or on an analysis of the incomes of in-migrants, out-migrants, and continuing residents. Insight into Boston's future can also be provided by an analysis of households employed in the city of Boston but residing in suburban apartments. Such an analysis is conducted in this chapter with the sample of suburban apartments used in the simulation of residential location decisions in Chapters 5 and 6. All the suburban apartments in this sample are located on or beyond a circumferential highway (Route 128) that is twelve to eighteen miles from the center of Boston. All the apartments in this sample and the BRA survey have been constructed since 1960.

A comparison of the tenant characteristics of these suburban and central city apartments shows that the central city tenants have higher incomes, are older, and have fewer children and smaller families than their suburban counterparts (Table 7-1). Since all of these apartments have been and continue to be advertised in the major Boston newspapers, it is no surprise to see them serving as a "port of entry" with a third or more of their tenants coming from outside the metropolitan area. At the same time, the suburban apartments have more tenants that are in-migrants to the Boston SMSA than do the central city apartments. In fact, 27 percent of the suburban households have moved from out-of-state residences. Nearly all (87.1 percent) of the 544 central-city apartment dwellers with jobs work in the central city; the remainder work in the suburbs. Barely half (56.3 percent) of the 2571 suburban apartment dwellers with jobs work in the suburbs; 31.9 percent work in the central city, and the remainder work in cities and towns adjacent to, but outside of, the SMSA.

Since only 12.5 percent of all the workers residing in the towns containing the suburban apartments in my sample worked in the city of Boston in 1970, the high percentage (31.9 percent) of suburban apartment residents working in the central city is unexpected.[6] Even more surprising is that 597, or nearly three-quarters, of the 819 suburban apartment residents working in the central city work in the central business district. Only 2.9 percent of all the workers in these towns worked in the Boston CBD in 1970. Since there were no apartments in these outer suburbs ten years ago, the large number of employed apartment dwellers now living in these towns and working in the central city (819 out of 2571), and the fact that 288 of them have no children and have annual incomes of $15,000 or more, indicates that some of Hoover and Vernon's centrally employed, childless, high-income households are now choosing apartments in the outer suburbs over apartments in the central city or central business district. In my sample of suburban apartment dwellers, 610 households have no children and work in the city of Boston. Although a large number of these households (288) have high annual incomes ($15,000 or more), the proportion with high incomes (47.2 percent) is below that for childless households living in the apartments sampled by the BRA (59.2 percent). Lower income (mostly $10,000 to $15,000 annually) families with jobs in the city of Boston and no children appear more likely to choose modern suburban apartments over modern central city apartments than their higher income counterparts. Of course, this curious situation could be caused by the unrepresentative nature of both samples; that is, the samples are not representative, in a statistical sense, of new, good, apartment housing in the central city and the outer suburbs.

Table 7-1

The Percentage Distribution of Several Household Characteristics for Suburban and Central City Apartment Dwellers: 1970

Household Characteristics	BRA Survey of CBD Apartment Dwellers	Author's Survey of Suburban Apartment Dwellers	
		All Households	Households with Jobs in the City of Boston
Household Income			
All Incomes	100.0	100.0	100.0
Less than $10,000	17.1	25.5	18.4
$10,000-$14,999	23.7	34.3	34.9
$15,000 or more	59.2	40.2	46.6
Age of Head (Years)			
All Ages	100.0	100.0	100.0
Under 30	30.9	42.1	48.8
30-59	45.4	47.7	46.8
60 or more	23.7	10.3	4.4
Household Size (Persons)			
All Sizes	100.0	100.0	100.0
1	47.4	27.2	21.4
2	41.4	48.9	52.6
3	7.0	14.6	15.3
4	4.2	7.6	8.9
5 or more	–	1.7	1.7
Percentage of Households with Children	0.9	24.4	24.7
Prior Residence Location			
All Locations	100.0	100.0	100.0
City of Boston	36.2	13.1	23.6
Elsewhere in Boston SMSA	31.6	44.0	36.4
Outside Boston SMSA	32.1	41.9	38.7
Not Reported	–	1.0	1.3
Head's Place of Work –Employed Households			
All Locations	100.0	100.0	100.0
City of Boston	87.1	31.9	100.0
Elsewhere in Boston SMSA	12.9	56.3	0.0
Outside SMSA	–	11.8	0.0

Table 7-1 (cont.)

Household Characteristics	BRA Survey of CBD Apartment Dwellers	Author's Survey of Suburban Apartment Dwellers	
		All Households	Households with Jobs in the City of Boston
Occupation of Head			
All Occupations	100.0	100.0	100.0
Professional	NA	40.4	47.6
Managers	NA	20.6	22.4
Sales Workers	NA	10.0	9.9
Clerical	NA	5.8	5.4
Other Occupations	NA	13.1	9.8
Retired	14.0	7.2	0.0
Students	NA	2.9	5.0

The information in Table 7-1 shows that households living in suburban apartments and working in the central city have slightly higher incomes, are slightly younger, and have more members in occupations classified as professional or managerial than suburban apartment residents as a whole. At the same time, suburban tenants do not differ in family size, presence of children, and prior residential location on the basis of place of work. The intriguing question, which was also raised in Chapter 5, is: why are households commuting more than thirty minutes one-way from work to the outer suburbs and choosing apartments instead of single-family houses? If they are going to live in an apartment, why not select one closer to or in the city of Boston where they work? The behavior of the 25 percent of these households with children is easier to understand than that of the remainder. Children in the family usually cause parents to desire open space and lower density living arrangements. Centrally located modern high-rise apartments do not provide these amenities but these suburban apartments do provide them. Suburban apartments often have large tracts of open land surrounding the apartments and provide various recreational facilities for children (tot lots, baseball diamonds, etc.) and parents (swimming pools, tennis courts, etc.). Two possible reasons why households without children are selecting apartments over single-family houses in the suburbs are 1) they are recent in-migrants to the metropolitan area who are renting while they are looking at the area's housing market with a view to buying a house; 2) they may want a single-family house but their incomes or assets are insufficient to carry the debt service and other expenses associated with the house and neighborhood of their choice, or the uncertainty about their future (e.g., job stability and location of job) is great enough that they are reluctant to make the commitments associated with buying a house.

Some of the centrally employed households living in suburban apartments may just be starting their careers but trying to live as close to the average level of housing consumption of their occupational counterparts as their lower current incomes and available assets (down-payment money) will allow. This explanation applies to households with and without children. It implies that these household heads are young, probably professionals or managers, and consuming more housing than their cash-flow income would allow them by making rather large value of time in commuting expenditures (a noncash flow). They would probably be renting in any case, but if they were to rent in Cambridge or in Boston, the amenities (tennis courts, swimming pools, etc.) available in apartment developments in Norwood or Framingham would make the rents for similar units at these central locations beyond their budget. For example, a young attorney might receive $13,000 annually. An amenity rich two-bedroom apartment in Boston would cost between $375 and $500 per month (Prudential Apartments or Harbor Towers) depending on size, height, and view, while a two-bedroom town house with swimming pool, tennis courts, basketball court, tot lot, and private courtyards rents for $285 per month (including parking) in Framingham. Under the first option at $400 per month for rent plus $50 per month for parking, the young lawyer would be spending 41.5 percent of his (her) cash flow gross income for rent and under the latter he (she) would be spending 26.3 percent. If he (she) already owns a car and plans to retain it at either location, the marginal out-of-pocket commuting costs from Framingham would probably be less than $390 per year or 3 percent of his (her) gross income, which would leave a substantial cash flow difference (12.2 percent) favoring Framingham. Not all households working in the central city would want to consume this bundle. Some might sacrifice amenities and interior space for a status location such as Beacon Hill.

Centrally employed households may also select suburban apartments because they want to minimize contact with the congestion, air pollution, and high crime rates (actual or perceived) that are found in the central city. In the words of an advertisement, they want to live in the midst of "more than 100 acres of rolling greenbelt—trees and meadows to wander and picnic in, paths for walking, jogging and bicycling."[7] Or as another advertisement puts it:

Hundreds of acres of woods and fields unroll before you . . . walking, bicycling, cross-country skiing trails . . . space for your own garden . . . picnic and barbecue sites. . . .
  Warm contemporary buildings welcome you . . . clustered among winding greenbelts, mature trees, old stone fences. . . .[8]

As these typical advertisements illustrate, the owners and managers are emphasizing low-density apartments accompanied by open space for recreational activities in clean "country" air. Perhaps these households seek to be closer to the earth, and the suburban apartment boom is in part the transfer of the themes accompanying single-family housing and homeownership in the 1950s to the rental submarket.

Without a detailed and carefully administered attitude survey, it is impossible to measure the importance of these various explanations. Since such a survey is among the most difficult to conduct with a high degree of validity and reliability, we may never know for sure. However, it is clear that the suburbs, including the outer suburbs involving one-half hour to one hour one-way commutes to work, are successfully competing with the central city to provide luxury apartments. At the same time there is a viable luxury apartment market in the central city, and it is playing an important part in the local economy.

8

Some Additional Policy Implications

Restrictive zoning practices and the future of apartments in central cities are issues of public policy that have been discussed in earlier chapters. The implications of suburban apartment development for transportation planning, public facility planning, local tax revenues, and racial desegregation are discussed in this chapter.

Transportation

An important part of transportation planning is the forecasting of intraurban travel demands. In general, transportation engineers and planners make land-use projections, estimate trip generation as a function of the type and intensity of land use, develop interzonal flows using a gravity model or an intervening opportunities model, estimate modal choice, and assign the projected travel demand to existing and planned highway and transit networks.[1] This procedure does not adequately incorporate feedback between transportation and urban development; it focuses on a static view of urban land use and transportation systems. If transportation planners were informed in advance that a large number of multifamily housing units would be constructed in each metropolitan area over the following ten years, their land-use forecasts would probably inaccurately predict the spatial distribution of these units within each metropolitan area. Prior to the suburban apartment boom, nearly all of the projected increase in multifamily housing would have been forecast for central locations and at higher densities than those actually constructed. As a result, their forecasts of travel demand and modal choice would have been inaccurate. Projecting the future is not an easy task. One of the failings of the traditional approach in transportation planning is that several parts of the process, notably the gravity and the intervening opportunities models, assume that the price (rent or value) of any given housing bundle is spatially invariant. Introducing the concept of "gross price" (the sum of housing price and household transport costs), wherever transport costs appear, would make these projection techniques more realistic. Such a modification is becoming increasingly feasible because of recent research activity focused on estimating gross price functions in several metropolitan areas including Boston, Chicago, Detroit, Pittsburgh, and San Francisco.[2]

The recent upsurge in multifamily housing should not be mistaken as a justification for rail rapid transit solutions to urban transportation problems. A very large proportion of these new apartments are located in the suburbs and are somewhat uniformly distributed throughout each metropolitan area. Figure 8-1 illustrates the spatial distribution of the new multifamily housing constructed during the 1960s in the cities and towns of the six counties in or adjacent to the Boston SMSA. Only the cities of Boston (23.1 percent) and Cambridge (5.1 percent) show more than 5 percent of the total. The distribution of the workplaces of the residents of suburban apartments are dispersed throughout the metropolitan area. The work-trip destinations of households in my sample of suburban apartments in the Boston metropolitan area are summarized in Table 8-1. In general, their work trips are concentrated in the subarea of residence, which reflects the role of the suburbanization of jobs in the demand for suburban apartments. At the same time, there is a strong but not dominant flow of work trips to the Boston central business district. However, these centrally employed workers come from widely scattered residence locations. Furthermore, a sizeable number of work trips have destinations outside the subarea of residence or the city of Boston; this is particularly evident for the apartments in Norwood and Beverly. In addition, most of these new apartment developments have low population densities. For these reasons, suburban apartment development is unlikely to generate the corridor volumes necessary to make rail transit an efficient transportation solution.

John Meyer, John Kain, and Martin Wohl have studied the relative costs of alternative transportation systems or modes of travel and have concluded that "rail transit remains economically attractive for the line-haul only where population densities are extremely high, facilities are to be constructed underground, or rail roadbed structures are already on hand and can be regarded as sunk costs.."[3] Some urban planners, however, contend that a rail transit system will lead to the construction of housing at the densities necessary to make the system cost effective. Available information indicates that land use, in a broad sense, in urban areas is independent of the availability of public transit. American urban areas have been decentralizing and developing at lower densities with or without rapid transit.[4] Although one can find examples of new high-density apartment developments near commuter railroad stations in the suburbs, that pattern is not widespread and is most common in the New York metropolitan area. For example, several high-density apartment buildings (high-rise structures with little open land except for parking) are located within walking distance of the commuter railroad station in Mt. Kisco, a New York suburb in upper Westchester County. On the other hand, a large apartment development in Boston's outer suburbs, which negotiated the location of a special commuter train station on its site bordering an existing commuter line, contains 700 apartments in garden style buildings (three-stories) and 200 town-house apartments on sixty acres for a low density of fifteen units per acre.

Most central city mayors are interested in retaining or attracting as residents

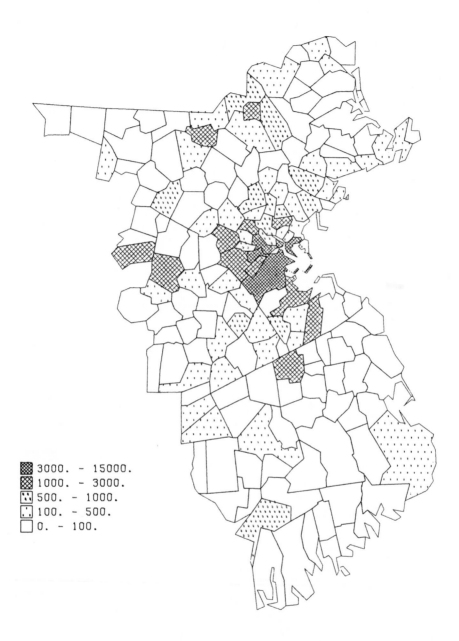

Figure 8-1. New Housing Units in Structures with Five or More Units By City and Town in the Six Counties in the Boston Region: 1960-70.

Table 8-1
The Distribution of Workplaces by Residence Location for Author's Survey of Suburban Apartment Residents: 1972

	Residence Locations													Total
	Boston SMSA								Worcester SMSA		Brockton SMSA		Providence SMSA	
	Middlesex County—Outer Ring				Norfolk County—Outer Ring		Essex County		Suburban Ring		Central City / Suburban Ring		Suburbs in Mass.	
Workplace	Framingham	Reading	Waltham	Woburn	Norwood	Weymouth	Beverly	Danvers	Shrewsbury	Westborough	Brockton	Bridgewater	Franklin	
Boston SMSA														
Central Business District of Boston	52	5	165	22	199	47	73	8	1	2	7	9	7	597
Remainder of the City of Boston	24	0	56	5	78	23	19	0	0	4	11	2	0	222
Remainder of Suffolk County	1	1	5	0	0	0	8	1	0	0	0	0	0	16
Middlesex County—Inner Ring[a]	23	4	113	19	65	7	19	4	0	3	3	1	5	266
Middlesex County—Outer Ring[a]	98	13	191	69	37	4	32	6	4	6	1	2	7	470
Norfolk County—Inner Ring[a]	10	0	18	2	98	18	2	0	1	1	15	8	7	180
Norfolk County—Outer Ring[a]	16	1	11	1	135	32	1	1	0	1	11	12	15	237
Essex County	0	1	6	1	2	1	127	37	0	0	0	0	0	175
Plymouth County	0	0	1	0	3	5	0	0	0	0	0	0	0	9
Worcester SMSA														
City of Worcester	3	0	0	0	1	0	1	0	26	9	0	0	1	41
Suburban Ring	1	0	1	0	0	0	0	0	14	3	0	0	1	20
Brockton SMSA														
City of Brockton	1	0	2	0	1	3	0	0	0	0	29	14	0	50
Suburban Ring	1	0	0	0	4	3	0	0	0	0	11	21	0	40
Providence SMSA														
Portion in Rhode Island	1	0	0	0	9	1	0	0	0	0	1	0	2	14
Portion in Massachusetts	0	0	0	0	5	1	0	0	0	0	1	0	14	21
Other Locations	9	1	20	9	21	2	22	1	2	6	13	7	5	120
Missing Information or Unemployed	61	4	35	25	123	35	92	7	8	10	34	27	30	491
Total	301	30	624	153	781	182	396	65	56	45	137	103	94	2967

[a]The inner ring of a county includes the cities and towns that are within that county and adjacent to the geographical boundary of the central city. The outer ring of a county includes the remaining cities and towns that are in that county and inside the SMSA.

the middle- and high-income households employed in their cities. Extending rail transit into suburban areas could be counterproductive from their point of view because it would reduce the time and out-of-pocket costs of commuting to a suburban apartment, which is accompanied by many amenities not found in the central city. Since housing and journey-to-work trips are complementary goods, it would not be surprising to see high-income central city workers switching to suburban apartments upon completion of rail transit extensions to the outer suburbs. The statistics on place of work for the sample of Boston suburban apartments analyzed in Chapter 7 indicate that a sizable number of middle- and high-income central city workers are already commuting to live in suburban apartments. Data gathered by the author on some of the Mt. Kisco apartment buildings shows that 25.3 percent of the households at work commute to Manhattan. In addition, 27.0 percent of the workers in the Boston development with its own railroad station work in the Boston central business district.

These factors do not mean that rail transit and other modes of public transportation should be avoided; they may produce social benefits and reduce social costs not included in calculations of cost effectiveness such as those of Meyer, Kain, and Wohl. The most common argument in favor of public transit is that it will reduce the health hazards accompanying automobile produced smog. If unrealized expectations regarding post-transit land use and the subsidy requirements of public transit are to be avoided, we must remember that decisions to expand public transit into the outer suburban areas, such as those currently under consideration in the Boston region including rail transit extensions, are based on environmental grounds and not on notions of cost effectiveness.

Sewer Facilities

Septic tanks, which are widely used in the outer suburbs, are inadequate to serve the population density accompanying apartment development. As a result, developers attempt to locate their apartment developments near existing sewer lines that connect to sewage treatment facilities. This dependency on sewer facilities raises two issues. First, how should local and state governments evaluate the growing number of developer proposals to install private sewage disposal facilities as part of their developments. Towns that lack any public sewage disposal and treatment facilities probably do not have employees who are trained to evaluate the health and safety features of these proposals. Since the construction of inadequate sewage treatment facilities can produce long-lived negative externalities, state governments should establish statewide performance standards for sewage treatment facilities and a bureau to administer the standards. The state might also want to restrict apartment development to areas that will be adequately served at the time the apartments will be occupied. This leads to the second issue, which stems from a growing awareness among suburban residents that sewers and sewage treatment facilities are a forerunner of apartments and urbanization.[5] Traditionally, single-family suburban home-owners have urged their governments to establish and extend sewer facilities. The future, however, may see local governments and their residents relying exclusively on septic tanks with a view to excluding apartment development and forestalling urbanization. Such behavior is especially likely on the part of some communities because zoning ordinances that exclude apartments have begun to receive unfavorable treatment when challenged in the courts.[6] In fact, there is already a large degree of overlap between towns in the Boston metropolitan area with restrictive zoning practices and those that lack public sewer facilities. It is not clear how the same courts will view the unavailability of sewer facilities, which have the effect of excluding apartments, when the zoning law is not prohibitive. If the states adopt standards for private sewage systems and issue licenses for their operation, the use of sewers to exclude apartments could be eliminated. Although several towns are interested in excluding apartments, the simulations of residential location decisions in Chapter 6 indicate that zoning regulations and/or the lack of public sewer facilities do not always prevent apartment development because of the strength of the forces behind the suburbanization of multifamily housing. Other studies of suburban apartments have also concluded that private developers of apartments often win their zoning battles.[7] If, however, a community seeking to exclude apartments is located near one or more communities that allow apartments, it has a higher probability of achieving its objective.

Fiscal Implications

Communities frequently debate the question of whether apartments cost local governments more in added services than they add to revenues. Most studies show that apartments, even at low densities, pay more in taxes and service charges than they cost in additional services (police and fire protection, garbage collection, sewers, water, recreational facilities, and education). These studies usually compare a single-family housing development with an apartment devel-opment covering the same acreage, and their conclusions are dependent on the assumption that apartments generate fewer school-age children. For example, one recent study assumed that each single-family house generated 2.4 school-age children while each apartment unit generated 0.6 school-age children.[8] The costs of other public services per dwelling unit are generally assumed to be the same for apartments and single-family housing units.

The survey of residents of apartments located in Boston's outer suburbs provides information that can be used to evaluate the assumptions underlying these studies of fiscal incidence. As a first step, we examine the stage in the family life cycle of the households in this sample. Twenty-two stages in the family life cycle have been defined on the basis of marital status, age of head, and age of children in the same manner as in Chapter 3. The distribtuion of the suburban apartment households across these stages is summarized in Table 8-2. The types of households living in these suburban apartments closely parallel the results of Chapter 3's analysis of the demand for apartments. In Chapter 3, households with children were the least likely to select an apartment, and only 18 percent of the households in the Boston survey of suburban apartments had children. Over half of the suburban apartment residents were either single (that is, never married) or young marrieds with no children. Married, divorced, or separated households with heads between the ages of 30 and 60 and with no

Table 8-2

Stages in the Family Life Cycle for Suburban Apartment Residents: Boston, 1972 (Author's Survey)

Stage in the Family Life Cycle	Number of Households
Single, under 30	561
Single, 30-60	361
Single, 60 or over	25
Married, No Children, under 30	534
Married, No Children, 30-60	399
Married, with Children, under 30	202
Married, Youngest Child under 6, 30-60	110
Married, Youngest Child 6 or over, 30-60	137
Married, with Children, 60 or over	1
Married, No Children, 60 or over	134
Widowhood, with Children, 60 or over	0
Widowhood, No Children, 60 or over	95
Widowhood, with Children, 30-60	9
Widowhood, No Children, 30-60	26
Widowhood, with Children, under 30	4
Widowhood, No Children, under 30	22
Divorced or Separated, with Children, 60 or over	0
Divorced or Separated, No Children, 60 or over	18
Divorced or Separated, with Children, 30-60	55
Divorced or Separated, No Children, 30-60	168
Divorced or Separated, with Children, under 30	19
Divorced or Separated, No Children, under 30	44
Missing Information	44
Total	2968

children were the next largest group. Most of the households with children were either young marrieds or middle-aged marrieds with young children. Consequently, a low incidence of school-age children per apartment appears to be a reasonable assumption. In fact, the average number of school-age children per household in this Boston sample is 0.137 (Table 8-3), a figure well below the value of 0.6 employed in the above study. The only value close to 0.6 is the 0.736 for three-bedroom, town-house apartments. Each apartment in a town-house apartment development contains two interior floors and has other apartments adjacent to it but none above or below it. In addition, each town-house apartment is usually accompanied by a small area of land adjacent to the unit and available for private as opposed to common use. The garden-style apartment consists of two-to-four story buildings, which contain apartments that have floor area on only one floor or level. The semi-town-house apartment is a combination of these two types of structure: that is, it contains apartments with two interior floors, but part of each apartment may be above or below another one and there is either less or no exterior private space. The high-rise apartment building is a tall building containing apartments that have their floor area on only one floor. All of these suburban apartments are accompanied by a generous amount of common open space. Of the four types of apartment structures in Table 8-3, the town house is closest in characteristics to low-density, single-family housing. As such, it might be expected to attract more families with school-age children than the other structure types, which is consistent with the data in Table 8-3. The town-house apartments have 0.333 school-age children per unit, while the semi-town-house apartments have 0.104 and the garden-style and high-rise units have 0.068.

To complete an evaluation of the assumptions about school-age children per household in studies of the fiscal incidence of apartments, we need to compare the number of school-age children per household in all types of structures. The public use samples of the *1970 Census of Population* provide the information to

Table 8-3

Average Number of School-Age Children per Apartment by Type of Structure and Number of Bedrooms: Boston, 1972 (Author's Survey)

| Type of Structure | Number of Bedrooms | | | |
	1	2	3	Total
Town-house	0.029	0.227	0.736	0.333
Semi-town-house	0.0	0.019	0.311	0.104
Garden-style	0.004	0.150	NA	0.068
High-rise	0.0	0.100	NA	0.067
Total	0.005	0.157	0.507	0.137
NA—not available				

make these comparisons for each metropolitan area in the United States. Comparisons for the Boston urbanized area are summarized in Table 8-4. It is not surprising that the variation in the average number of school-age children per household is largely due to the variation in the number of bedrooms and not to the type of structure. Single-family houses can be assigned a larger number of school-age children per household than apartments because on average single-family houses contain more bedrooms per unit (usually three or four) than apartments (usually one or two). In view of the data in Tables 8-3 and 8-4, a figure between 1.2 and 1.9 school-age children per unit for single-family housing and one of 0.2 school-age children per unit for apartments probably constitute a valid set of assumptions for comparing the fiscal impacts of apartments with those of single-family houses. Since any specific developer proposal will include the exact distribution of apartments by number of bedrooms, an accurate comparison to the jurisidiction's single-family houses will be possible using the information in Table 8-4.

The recreational facilities provided by many suburban apartment developments suggests that there may be a shift in demand away from public provision of parks and recreation facilities. New condominium housing developments and even some tracts of single-family housing also include open space, tennis courts, swimming pools, and other recreation facilities including a social director and

Table 8-4

The Average Number of School-Age Children per Household by Age of Structure, Type of Structure, and Number of Bedrooms: Boston, 1970

Age and Type of Structure	Number of Bedrooms					
	Efficiency	1	2	3	4	5
New Buildings (1960-1970)						
Single-Family Houses	NA	0.0	0.400	1.153	1.913	3.259
Two-Family Houses	NA	0.0	0.258	0.762	NA	NA
Garden-Style Apartments	0.0	0.016	0.112	0.955	NA	NA
High-Rise Apartments	0.0	0.052	0.226	NA	NA	NA
Total	0.0	0.023	0.197	1.119	1.913	3.259
Older Buildings (before 1960)						
Single-Family Houses	0.167	0.064	0.224	0.963	1.578	2.070
Two-Family Houses	0.0	0.041	0.261	1.011	1.932	1.531
Garden-Style Apartments	0.017	0.034	0.310	1.130	2.133	1.900
High-Rise Apartments	0.0	0.0	0.250	1.167	NA	NA
Total	0.020	0.037	0.232	0.989	1.710	2.007

NA—not available

Source: U.S. Bureau of the Census, *One-in-a-100: A Public Use Sample of the 1970 Census* (the 5 percent neighborhood characteristics file for the Boston urbanized area).

other social functions. If such a shift is occurring, local governments may be freed from the costs of providing recreational services in the face of increasing demand.

Racial Desegregation

Racial discrimination in the housing market has made it very difficult for black households to obtain housing outside the ghetto.[9] Discrimination in other areas, especially employment and wages, has made it difficult for blacks to afford a single-family house of their own, which in turn has closed numerous suburban housing markets to them.[10] Henry Terrell's analysis of the *1967 Survey of Economic Opportunity* (SEO) shows

that urban white families had a mean net worth (all assets minus all debts) of $20,874 compared to a net worth of only $3,362 for urban black families. Although asset and liability data are unreliable due to response errors, these data appear quite convincing in showing that urban black families have only roughly one-sixth the net worth of urban white families. This disparity in net worth is substantially greater than can be explained by income alone since net accumulation of black families is less than one-half of white accumulation at all income levels. The data on net worth from the SEO show clearly that income data alone understate the real economic position of black families by not accounting for their relatively poorer net worth position.[11]

It is no surprise that few blacks have been able to live in suburban communities that consist of single-family, owner-occupied housing; their asset position severely restricts their ability to make the necessary down payments. The suburbanization of multifamily housing has made high-quality housing without down-payment requirements available in many of these same communities. One result should be easier black access to these suburban housing markets and in turn to suburban jobs.

9   Summary

The large role of apartments in new construction since 1957 is largely explained by the substantial increase in the types of households that have traditionally consumed them. Young, single households and young, married, childless households have increased in number and as a share of the population since the mid-1950s, and the analysis in Chapter 3 shows that households in these stages of the family life cycle are very likely to choose an apartment. At the same time, rising land costs, high demolition and disaster losses, and the suburbanization of employment have augmented these changes in the composition of the population and have added fuel to the boom in apartment construction. Possibly the most interesting aspect of the growth in multifamily housing has been the high proportion of apartments built in the suburbs. This shift in the location of multifamily housing within metropolitan areas reflects in large part the suburbanization of employment. The development of suburban employment centers has attracted apartments much like the demand for apartments that accompanied central city employment concentrations in the nineteenth and early twentieth centuries. Statistical analyses of the probability of residing in a suburban apartment indicate that suburban workers are more likely to choose this type of residential accommodation than are central city workers. At the same time, the offspring of the suburban single-family homeowners probably want to live in neighborhoods similar to the ones where they grew up but cannot afford to rent or buy single-family houses. As a result, they rent suburban apartments. In addition there is reason to believe that during the 1950s an excess supply of good quality apartments in the central city limited the profitability of suburban apartment development and delayed the adjustment to these factors. But as the stock of central city apartments has deteriorated and grown obsolete, the excess supply of good central city apartments has declined and suburban construction of these units has become profitable. A simple econometric model of the suburbanization of apartments in Chapter 4 generally supports these hypotheses.

The aggregate statistical analyses of the demand for apartments and the response of the supply in large metropolitan areas is supplemented by more detailed analyses of suburban apartments in the Boston metropolitan area (Chapter 5). These analyses show that households living in these new suburban apartment units place a high value on adult recreation facilities (tennis courts and function rooms but not swimming pools), security (guards and other protective devices) and a panoramic view of hills or water. Playgrounds,

119

swimming pools, and social directors are valued negatively; that is, they reduce the value of the apartment in the average consumer's eyes.

A simulation of the housing choices of 2800 Boston suburban renters provides general support for the hypothesis that households select the residential location that minimizes their total location costs (gross price of housing), which is the sum of house price (rent) and commuting costs. Forty-three percent of the households choose a residential location that was one of the 15 cheapest of the 122 available sites. Households with suburban jobs scored even higher with 65 percent selecting one of the 15 cheapest locations. These simulations also show that restrictive zoning ordinances and the lack of public sewer facilities have some retarding effect on apartment development. However, there are many exceptions, and several towns have restrictive practices that are not binding. That is, there is no consumer demand for apartments located in these towns.

The Future Demand for Multifamily Housing

Since demographic change is a major factor in explaining the multifamily housing boom, the steady decline in the birth rate over the last fifteen years inevitably leads to questions about the market for multifamily housing in the future. One consequence of the decline in the birth rate is that the number of households in the stage of the family life cycle most likely to select an apartment (single and under thirty years of age) will probably begin to decrease roughly twenty years after the first signs of a decline in the birth rate. Projections of the population categorized by stages in the family life cycle would be most suitable for an analysis of this question. Unfortunately, the only projections available are the Bureau of the Census' projections of the population categorized by age. The projection relying on a birth rate of 2.1 (average number of births per woman upon completion of child-bearing) is summarized in Table 9-1. The number of persons in the twenty to twenty-nine years age group is projected to increase until the early 1980s, but it then starts a decline which is projected to continue until the year 2000. At the same time, the number of persons in those age groups (thirty to sixty years) that are likely to be in a stage of the family life cycle that has been shown to prefer single-family houses over apartments should increase through most of the next thirty years with decline becoming evident in the year 2000. These patterns suggest an increase in the demand for single-family houses until 2000 and continued growth in the demand for multifamily housing until the early 1980s. If, however, fewer households have children in the future, the shift to single-family houses would be less. Several factors prevent confident assertions about the future demand by structure type. For example, if marriages decline while the number of primary individuals increases, or if marriage rates remain constant but households tend to

Table 9-1

Projection of Population by Age: 1972-2000 (Millions)

Age	Year						
	1972	1975	1980	1985	1990	1995	2000
All Ages	208.8	213.9	224.1	235.7	246.6	256.0	264.4
Under 5	17.2	16.8	18.6	20.7	20.5	19.5	19.2
5-9	18.7	17.3	16.9	18.7	20.7	20.7	19.7
10-14	20.8	20.1	17.5	17.1	18.9	20.9	20.8
15-19	20.1	20.9	20.2	17.7	17.3	19.1	21.0
20-24	18.2	19.4	21.1	20.4	17.8	17.4	19.2
25-29	15.0	17.3	19.5	21.2	20.5	18.0	17.6
30-34	12.3	13.8	17.4	19.6	21.3	20.6	18.1
35-39	11.1	11.6	13.8	17.4	19.6	21.3	20.6
40-44	11.6	11.1	11.5	13.7	17.3	19.5	21.1
45-49	12.0	11.8	11.0	11.4	13.5	17.0	19.2
50-54	11.6	11.8	11.5	10.7	11.1	13.2	16.6
55-59	10.2	10.6	11.2	10.9	10.2	10.6	12.6
60-64	8.9	9.2	9.9	10.4	10.2	9.5	9.9
65-69	7.2	7.7	8.2	8.8	9.3	9.1	8.5
70-74	5.6	5.9	6.5	6.9	7.4	7.9	7.6
75 or over	8.1	8.6	9.4	10.2	11.0	11.8	12.6
Median age (Years)	28.1	28.6	29.6	30.6	31.8	33.0	34.0

Source: U.S. Bureau of the Census, *Current Population Reports: Population Estimates and Projections*, Series P-25, No. 493 (December 1972), Table 2 (Series E).

delay having children, the multifamily housing market would probably benefit. The population projections in Table 9-1 also show an increase in the elderly population, a segment that prefers multifamily housing more than households that have children but not as much as single young persons. Since the type and location of multifamily dwelling units that the elderly might demand probably differ from those being built for never married persons and young married couples with no children, the effect of this growing age group on the demand for housing, in particular as a source of replacement demand for much of the new multifamily housing, is obscure.

Several economic and social factors also threaten to make a mockery of any predictions. Real incomes seem likely to continue to increase over the next thirty years, and such increases are generally expected to generate an increase in the demand for single-family houses. On the other hand, the ownership of multifamily housing units as condominiums may quench the thirst to own one's home that accompanies higher incomes. In addition, since the number of working wives is increasing, households may spend less time in their homes, a trend which should favor multifamily housing. Delaying the arrival of children, which also seems to be popular, probably has the same effect. On the price side of the picture, if single-family houses continue to increase in price, more and more consumers will be priced out of that market and into the multifamily housing submarket. Although any one or more of these unpredictable events could render a prediction valueless, it does seem that the apartment market will at least level off in the early 1980s. Because of information lags, this should show up in a decline in the number of multifamily starts in 1986 or 1987.

Appendixes

Appendix A: Housing Starts: 1889-1971

| | Private Nonfarm Housing Starts (1000) | | | | Public Housing Starts (1000) | | Federally Insured Housing Starts (1000) | | |
Year	Total	Multi-family	Percent Multi-family	Mobile Homes	Total	Multi-family	FHA 1-4 Families	FHA Project Units	VA Homes
1889	342.0	NA							
1890	328.0	NA							
1891	298.0	NA							
1892	381.0	NA							
1893	267.0	NA							
1894	265.0	NA							
1895	309.0	NA							
1896	257.0	NA							
1897	292.0	NA							
1898	262.0	NA							
1899	282.0	NA							
1900	189.0	35.0	18.5						
1901	275.0	66.0	24.0						
1902	240.0	37.0	15.4						
1903	253.0	48.0	19.0						
1904	315.0	63.0	20.0						
1905	507.0	107.0	21.1						
1906	487.0	102.0	20.9						
1907	432.0	82.0	19.0						
1908	416.0	65.0	15.6						
1909	492.0	91.0	18.5						
1910	387.0	79.0	20.4						
1911	395.0	84.0	21.2						
1912	426.0	97.0	22.8						
1913	421.0	85.0	20.2						
1914	421.0	86.0	20.4						
1915	433.0	98.0	22.6						
1916	437.0	101.0	23.1						
1917	240.0	43.0	18.3						
1918	118.0	14.0	11.9						
1919	315.0	40.0	12.7						
1920	247.0	21.0	8.5						
1921	449.0	63.0	14.0						
1922	716.0	133.0	18.6						

Year	Private Nonfarm Housing Starts (1000)			Mobile Homes	Public Housing Starts (1000)		Federally Insured Housing Starts (1000)		
	Total	Multi-family	Percent Multi-family		Total	Multi-family	FHA 1-4 Families	FHA Project Units	VA Homes
1923	871.0	183.0	21.0						
1924	893.0	186.0	20.8						
1925	937.0	208.0	22.2						
1926	849.0	241.0	28.4						
1927	810.0	257.0	31.7						
1928	753.0	239.0	31.7						
1929	509.0	142.0	27.9						
1930	330.0	74.0	22.4						
1931	254.0	45.0	17.6						
1932	134.0	9.0	6.7						
1933	93.0	12.0	12.9						
1934	126.0	12.0	9.5						
1935	215.7	25.8	12.0		5.3	4.2	13	1	
1936	304.2	52.4	17.2		14.8	8.6	49	1	
1937	332.4	51.3	15.5		3.6	1.7	57	3	
1938	399.3	64.9	16.3		6.7	6.1	107	12	
1939	458.4	65.7	14.3		56.6	21.3	145	13	
1940	529.6	56.4	10.6		73.0	23.2	177	3	
1941	619.5	57.9	9.3		86.6	10.4	217	3	
1942	301.2	31.4	10.4		54.8	11.7	160	5	
1943	183.7	29.6	16.1		7.3	Z	126	20	
1944	138.7	13.5	9.7		3.1	Z	84	10	
1945	325.0	14.7	4.5		1.2	1.2	39	2	9
1946	1015.0	48.2	4.7		8.0	8.0	67	2	92
1947	1265.0	71.5	5.7		3.4	3.4	178	51	160
1948	1344.0	104.0	7.7		18.1	14.1	216	78	71
1949	1430.0	161.7	11.3		36.3	32.6	253	111	91
1950	1408.0	159.2	8.4		43.6	37.9	328	158	191
1951	1420.0	87.5	6.2		71.2	63.4	187	77	149
1952	1446.0	83.4	5.8		58.5	55.1	229	51	141
1953	1402.0	94.0	6.7		35.5	30.5	217	35	157
1954	1532.0	90.2	5.9		18.6	18.1	251	25	307
1955	1627.0	86.7	5.3		19.6	15.0	269	8	393
1956	1325.0	82.3	6.2	124.3	24.2	15.1	183	6	271
1957	1175.0	119.5	10.2	119.3	49.1	16.5	150	18	128
1958	1314.0	170.1	13.0	102.5	67.9	25.3	270	25	102
1959	1494.6	226.9	15.2	120.5	36.7	17.2	307	25	109

	Private Nonfarm Housing Starts (1000)				Public Housing Starts (1000)		Federally Insured Housing Starts (1000)		
Year	Total	Multi-family	Percent Multi-family	Mobile Homes	Total	Multi-family	FHA 1-4 Families	FHA Project Units	VA Homes
1960	1230.1	213.4	17.3	103.7	43.9	23.4	226	35	75
1961	1284.8	294.8	23.0	90.2	52.0	31.3	199	45	83
1962	1439.0	422.1	29.2	118.0	29.7	18.1	197	62	78
1963	1582.9	536.5	33.9	150.8	31.8	23.2	166	55	71
1964	1502.3	504.5	33.6	191.3	32.1	22.2	154	51	59
1965	1450.6	458.2	31.6	216.5	36.9	28.3	160	36	49
1966	1141.5	351.4	30.8	217.3	30.9	24.0	129	29	37
1967	1268.4	406.3	32.0	240.4	30.3	22.9	142	38	52
1968	1483.6	562.2	37.9	318.0	37.8	29.3	148	72	56
1969	1449.1	613.2	42.3	412.7	32.8	26.9	154	80	51
1970	1415.9	578.3	40.8	398.1	33.4	25.6	234	184	61
1971	2033.5	846.1	41.6	492.0	32.3	24.8	301	231	94

NA: Not Available

Z: Less than 50 units

Sources: U.S. Bureau of the Census, *Housing Construction Statistics: 1889-1964* (Washington, D.C.: U.S. Government Printing Office, 1966), Table A-2 (1889-1962); U.S. Bureau of the Census, *Construction Reports*, "Housing Starts" (September 1967), Series C20-67-7 (1963-July 1967); U.S. Bureau of the Census, *Construction Reports*, "Housing Starts," Series C20 (1967-1971); Grebler, Blank, and Winnick, *Capital Formation in Residential Real Estate*, p. 147 (FHA data for 1935-1944); U.S. Department of Housing and Urban Development, *HUD Trends: Annual Summary*.

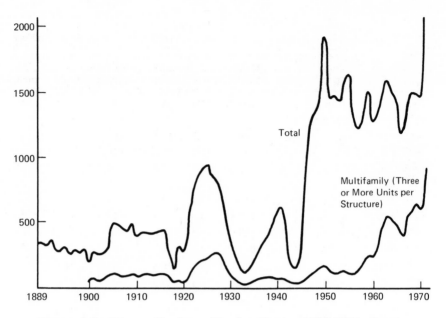

Figure A-1. Private Nonfarm Housing Starts: 1889-1971. Source: Appendix A.

Appendix B: List of Sixty-Three SMSAs Used in Tables 2-1 and 2-2

Akron
Allentown-Bethlehem-Easton
Baltimore
Birmingham
Boston
Bridgeport
Buffalo
Chattanooga
Chicago
Cincinnati
Cleveland
Dallas
Dayton
Denver
Des Moines
Detroit
Erie
Fort Wayne
Fort Worth
Fresno
Gary-Hammond-East Chicago
Grand Rapids
Greensboro-Winston Salem-
   High Point
Hartford
Houston
Indianapolis
Jersey City
Kansas City
Los Angeles-Long Beach
Louisville
Memphis

Miami, Florida
Milwaukee
Minneapolis-St. Paul
Newark
New Haven
New Orleans
New York
Norfolk-Portsmouth
Oklahoma
Omaha
Patterson-Clifton-Passaic
Peoria
Philadelphia
Phoenix
Pittsburgh
Providence-Pawtucket-Warwick
Rochester
Sacramento
St. Louis
Salt Lake City
San Antonio
San Diego
San Francisco-Oakland
San Jose
Seattle-Everett
Spokane
Springfield-Chicopee-Holyoke
Syracuse
Tacoma
Tampa-St. Petersburg
Tucson
Washington, D.C.

Appendix C: List of Sixty-Four SMSAs Used in Table 2-3 and Chapters 3 and 4

Akron
Albany-Schenectady-Troy
Allentown-Bethlehem-Easton
Anaheim-Santa Ana-Garden Grove
Atlanta
Baltimore
Birmingham
Boston
Buffalo
Chicago
Cincinnati
Cleveland
Columbus, Ohio
Dallas
Dayton
Denver
Detroit
Fort Lauderdale
Fort Worth
Gary-Hammond-East Chicago
Grand Rapids
Greensboro-Winston Salem
  High Point
Hartford
Houston
Indianapolis
Jacksonville
Jersey City
Kansas City
Los Angeles-Long Beach
Louisville
Memphis
Miami, Florida

Milwaukee
Minneapolis-St. Paul
Nashville-Davidson
Newark
New Orleans
New York
Norfolk-Portsmouth
Oklahoma
Omaha
Patterson-Clifton-Passaic
Philadelphia
Phoenix
Pittsburgh
Portland
Providence-Pawtucket-Warwick
Richmond
Rochester
Sacramento
St. Louis
Salt Lake City
San Antonio
San Bernardino-Riverside-Ontario
San Diego
San Francisco-Oakland
San Jose
Seattle-Everett
Springfield-Chicopee-Holyoke
Syracuse
Tampa-St. Petersburg
Toledo
Washington, D.C.
Youngstown-Warren

Notes

Notes

Chapter 1
Multifamily Housing: An Historical Perspective

1. L. Grebler, D.M. Blank, and L. Winnick, *Capital Formation in Residential Real Estate* (Princeton: Princeton University Press, 1956), p. 84.

2. Nelson N. Foote, Janet Abu-Lughod, Mary Mix Foley, and Louis Winnick, *Housing Choices and Housing Constraints* (New York: McGraw-Hill, 1960), pp. 283-85, 361-67.

3. See, e.g., Martin H. David, *Family Composition and Consumption* (Amsterdam: North Holland Publishing Company, 1962), pp. 53-81; U.S. Department of Housing and Urban Development, *Housing Surveys* (Washington, D.C.: Government Printing Office, 1969).

4. U.S. Breau of the Census, *Census of Housing: 1970, Metropolitan Housing Characteristics, United States and Regions*, Final Report HC(2)-1 (Washington, D.C.: Government Printing Office, 1972), Tables A-3, A-4, and A-7.

5. U.S. Bureau of the Census, *Census of Housing: 1970, Detailed Housing Characteristics, United States Summary*, Final Report (HC(1)-B1 (Washington, D.C.: Government Printing Office, 1972), Table 32; U.S. Bureau of the Census, *Census of Housing: 1960, States and Small Areas, United States Summary* (Washington, D.C.: Government Printing Office, 1963), Table 2.

6. Farm and nonfarm housing units are included in these figures because nonfarm multifamily data is not available. From 1960 to 1970, 7.72 million farm and nonfarm (combined) dwelling units and 1.57 million multifamily dwelling units (farm and nonfarm) were lost. Metropolitan area figures are not used because of changes in the number and boundaries of such areas. U.S. Bureau of the Census, *Census of Housing 1970, Metropolitan Housing Characteristics, United States and Regions*, Final Report HC(2)-1 (Washington, D.C.: Government Printing Office, 1972), Table A-6; U.S. Bureau of the Census, *Census of Housing: 1960, States and Small Areas*, Table 2.

7. The FHA data is based on units started under FHA inspection. This does not mean that they were financed under FHA programs, although this is a much better assumption for multifamily than for home (1 to 4 family structures) starts. The section 608 figure is based on units for which FHA insurance was written in that year. Housing and Home Finance Agency, *Historial Statistics* (1960); HUD, *Housing Statistics: Annual Data* (May 1966), Table A-6, p. 5; HUD, *HUD Trends: Annual Summary* (May 1969), Table A-7, p. 5.

8. See Sam Bass Warner, *Streetcar Suburbs* (New York: Atheneum, 1969).

9. See generally, E.M. Hoover and R. Vernon, *Anatomy of a Metropolis* (Cambridge, Mass.: Harvard University Press, 1959); R. Vernon, *The Changing*

Economic Function of the Central City (New York: Committee for Economic Development, 1959); J.R. Meyer, J.F. Kain, and Martin Wohl, *The Urban Transportation Problem* (Cambridge, Mass.: Harvard University Press, 1965); and L. Moses and H.F. Williamson, "The Location of Economic Activity," *American Economic Review* 57 (May 1967): 211-22.

10. U.S. Department of Commerce, *Construction Review* (December 1971), Table E-1, p. 48. (1957-59 equals 100 for both indexes.)

11. For example, Elsie Eaves, *How the Many Costs of Housing Fit Together* Research Report No. 16 to the National Commission on Urban Problems, Table 28, p. 52 (1969); Alan R. Winger and John Madden, "Application of the Theory of Joint Products: The Case of Residential Construction," *Quarterly Review of Economics and Business* 10 (Summer 1970): 61-69.

12. John P. Shelton, "The Cost of Renting versus Owning a Home," *Land Economics* 42 (February 1968), 59-72. For a discussion of the federal income tax law and housing, see Henry Aaron, "Income Taxes and Housing," *American Economic Review* 60 (December 1970): 789-806.

13. Louis Winnick, *Rental Housing: Opportunities for Private Investment* (New York: McGraw-Hill, 1958), p. 241.

Chapter 2
The Suburban Housing Market

1. Robert H. Haig, "Toward An Understanding of the Metropolis," *Quarterly Journal of Economics* 40 (May 1926): 402-34.

2. Much of this discussion is based on John F. Kain, "The Distribution and Movement of Jobs and Industry," in J.Q. Wilson, ed., *The Metropolitan Enigma* (New York: Doubleday, 1970).

3. Ibid., pp. 15-17. The data has been corrected for annexations and refers to the boundaries of the central cities and suburban rings as defined in 1950.

4. See John R. Meyer, John F. Kain, and Martin Wohl, *The Urban Transportation Problem* (Cambridge, Massachusetts: Harvard University Press, 1965), note 2, p. 27. Kain used actual annual population annexation figures to make his corrections. In the present case the annual annexation figures are assumed to be constant over 1960-70 and are estimated from the total amount of population annexed by the central city in the decade.

5. Andrew Marshall Hamer, *Industrial Exodus from Central City* (Lexington, Mass.: Lexington Books, D.C. Heath and Company, 1973), p. 32.

6. Ibid., p. 94.

7. William Alonso, *Location and Land Use* (Cambridge, Massachusetts: Harvard University Press, 1965); Edwin S. Mills, "An Aggregative Model of Resource Allocation in a Metropolitan Area," *American Economic Review* 57 (May 1967); Richard Muth, *Cities and Housing* (Chicago: University of Chicago

Press, 1969); Lowdon Wingo, Jr., *Transportation and Urban Land* (Washington, D.C.: Resources for the Future, 1961). See also R.N.S. Harris, G.S. Tolley, and C. Harrell, "The Residence Site Choice," *Review of Economics and Statistics* 50 (May 1968): 241-47.

8. Mahlon Straszheim, "Estimation of the Demand for Urban Housing Services from Household Interview Data," *Review of Economics and Statistics* 55 (February 1973): 4.

9. John F. Kain, "The Journey to Work as a Determinant of Residential Location," *Papers and Proceedings of the Regional Science Association* 9 (1962), 137-61.

10. Kain, "Distribution and Movement," Table 1.

11. U.S. Bureau of the Census, *Census of Housing: 1940* (Washington, D.C.: Government Printing Office, 1944); U.S. Bureau of the Census, *Census of Housing: 1950, Nonfarm Housing Characteristics*, vol. 2, pt. 1 (Washington, D.C.: Government Printing Office, 1954); U.S. Bureau of the Census, *Census of Housing: 1960, Metropolitan Housing*, vol. 2, pt. 1 (Washington, D.C.: Government Printing Office, 1963); U.S. Bureau of the Census, *Census of Housing: 1970, Metropolitan Housing Characteristics* (Washington, D.C.: Government Printing Office, 1972). These simple comparisons illustrate the difficulties in gathering historical evidence; they are troubled by changes in the definition and number of metropolitan areas over time, and by the alteration of the stock through demolitions and conversions.

12. Meyer, Kain, and Wohl, *Urban Transportation Problem*, p. 129.

13. Straszheim, "Estimation of the Demand." Reprinted with permission.

Chapter 3
The Demand for Multifamily Housing
in Metropolitan Areas

1. David Harrison, Jr. and John F. Kain, "Cumulative Urban Growth and Urban Density Functions," *Journal of Urban Economics* 1 (1974): 61-98. See also, David Harrison, Jr. and John F. Kain, "An Historical Model of Urban Form," Discussion Paper No. 63, Harvard University Program on Regional and Urban Economics (September 1970); and David Harrison, Jr., and John F. Kain, "Cumulative Urban Growth and Urban Density Functions," Discussion Paper No. 75, Harvard University Program on Regional and Urban Economics (February 1973).

2. Edwin S. Mills, *Studies in the Structure of the Urban Economy* (Baltimore: Johns Hopkins Press, 1972), pp. 48-49.

3. The first period was pre-1879, and it was assigned the value of 1.0. The remaining periods and their time values in parentheses are: 1880-89 (2.0); 1890-99 (3.0); 1900-1909 (4.0); 1910-19 (5.0); 1920-24 (5.5); 1925-29 (6.0);

1930-34 (6.5); 1935-39 (7.0); 1940-44 (7.5); 1945-49 (8.0); 1950-54 (8.5); 1955-60 (9.0). For the periods simulated in this chapter, the values are 9.5 for 1960-64 and 10.0 for 1965-70. Note that the Harrison-Kain models have a limited dependent variable, and hence their error terms are heteroscedastic; it does not appear that the authors made any efforts to correct this.

4. H. James Brown and John F. Kain, "Submarket Demand Functions for San Francisco" in *The NBER Urban Simulation Model*, vol. 2: *Supporting Empirical Studies*, ed. by John F. Kain (1971, mimeo), Chapter 3. See also Gregory K. Ingram, John F. Kain and J. Royce Ginn, *The Detroit Prototype of the NBER Urban Simulation Model* (New York: National Bureau of Economic Research, 1972), App. B.

5. For an early application of this approach see Guy H. Orcutt, Martin Greenberger, John Korbel, and Alice M. Rivlin, *Microanalysis of Socioeconomic Systems: A Simulation Study* (New York: Harper and Row, 1961).

6. Franklin J. James and James W. Hughes, *Economic Growth and Residential Patterns: A Methodological Investigation* (New Brunswick, New Jersey: Center for Urban Policy Research, Rutgers University, 1972), pp. 44, 45, 50-51.

7. Ibid., p. 51.

8. John B. Lansing and Leslie Kish, "Family Life Cycle as an Independent Variable," *American Sociological Review*, 22 (1957), 512-19.

9. The one-in-a-thousand sample contains the separate records of the characteristics of a 0.1 percent sample of the U.S. population as recorded in the 1960 census. For a detailed description of this data, see U.S. Bureau of the Census, *Censuses of Population and Housing: 1960. 1/1000 and 1/10,000: Two National Samples of the Population Of the United States—Description and Technical Documentation* (1964). There are two independently drawn 0.1 percent samples of the U.S. population in 1960. The second one was drawn to provide a 1960 data set comparable to the 1970 samples. U.S. Bureau of the Census, *One-in-a-100: A Public Use Sample of Basic Records from the 1960 Census: Description and Technical Documentation* (March 1971). The second one identifies the state of residence but does not identify the size of the SMSA. Since the probability functions are likely to vary with SMSA size, the first sample which identifies the size of the SMSA of residence was relied upon for the estimates.

10. The probability of selecting a suburban apartment is equal to a) the product of the probability of selecting an apartment and the probability of selecting the suburbs *given that* the household selects an apartment, or b) the product of the probability of selecting the suburbs and the probability of selecting an apartment *given that* the household selects the suburbs.

11. Since the dependent variable is dichotomous, the error term is heteroscedastic. As a result, the estimates of the coefficients are unbiased but the estimates of their variances are biased and inefficient. The prescribed approach is to estimate the coefficients using generalized least squares by transforming the variables by the square root of $1/\hat{P}(1 - \hat{P})$ where $\hat{P}$ is the predicted value of the dependent variable from OLS. However, if $\hat{P}$ is less than or equal to zero, or

greater than or equal to one, the weighting procedure breaks down. Any approach to handling these cases will produce quasi-generalized least-squares estimators which could be worse than OLS. In fact, some limited research indicates that they will be; see S.M. Goldfeld and R. Quandt, *Nonlinear Methods in Econometrics* (Amsterdam: North Holland Press, 1972), pp. 130-34. These authors also suggest that more sophisticated techniques such as probit analysis may not outperform OLS. Zellner appears more optimistic in the case of dependent variables that are proportions. A. Zellner, "An Efficient Method of Estimating Seemingly Unrelated Regressions and Tests for Aggregation Bias," *Journal of the American Statistical Association* 57 (June 1962): 348-68; A. Zellner and T.H. Lee, "Joint Estimation of Relationships Involving Discrete Random Variables," *Econometrica* 33 (April 1965), 382-94. In the present case, 2.3 percent of the observations have predicted values from the OLS that fall outside the range of the dependent variable. There are enough observations in each cell of the whole SMSA model for large SMSAs to calculate cell percentages that could be used to compare OLS and GLS estimates. (A series of independent variables which are dummies performs an analysis of variance by dividing the sample into cells.) The OLS estimates were much better predictors of the cell probabilities than the GLS estimates. See also D.S. Huang, *Regression and Econometric Methods* (New York: McGraw-Hill, 1970), pp. 169-71.

12. Two of the stages in the life cycle used in Table 3-2 were merged to overcome a problem of insufficient observations in the two categories; the divorced or separated, sixty or more years of age and the divorced, separated, or widowed, under thirty years of age categories were merged.

13. For the test, see Charles R. Frank, Jr., *Statistics and Econometrics* (New York: Holt, Rinehart and Winston, 1971), pp. 257-60.

14. Richard F. Muth, "The Demand for Non-Farm Housing," in *The Demand for Durable Goods*, ed. by Arnold C. Harberger (Chicago: University of Chicago Press, 1960), pp. 29-96.

15. P. Rao and R.L. Miller, *Applied Econometrics* (Belmont, California: Wadsworth Publishing Co., 1971), pp. 46-52.

16. U.S. Bureau of the Census, *Census of Housing: 1970, Metropolitan Housing Characteristics*, HC(2)-1 to 244 (Washington, D.C.: Government Printing Office, 1972), Tables A-7.

17. Muth, "Demand for Non-Farm Housing."

18. For example, with Muth's coefficient of adjustment, all but 3 percent of the excess of desired over actual stock for the first year will have been supplied by the end of the decade, and for the fifth year the figure is 21.7 percent.

Chapter 4
The Spatial Distribution of Multifamily Housing

1. John Niedercorn and John F. Kain, "An Econometric Model of Metropolitan Development," *Papers and Proceedings of the Regional Science Association* 11 (1963), 123-43.

2. Andrew Marshall Hamer, *Industrial Exodus from Central City: Public Policy and the Comparative Costs of Location* (Lexington, Mass.: Lexington Books, D.C. Heath and Company, 1973).

3. Neidercorn and Kain, "Econometric Model," p. 137.

4. U.S. Bureau of the Census, *Census of Population: 1970*, Vol. I: *Characteristics of the Population, Part A Number of Inhabitants, Section I: United States* (Washington, D.C.: Government Printing Office, 1972), Table 34; U.S. Bureau of the Census, *Census of Population: 1960* (Washington, D.C.: Government Printing Office, 1963); U.S. Bureau of the Census, *Census of Housing: 1970, Detailed Housing Characteristics, United States Summary* (Washington, D.C.: Government Printing Office, 1972), Table 39; U.S. Bureau of the Census, *Census of Housing: 1960*, vol. 1: *States and Small Areas, Part 1, U.S. Summary* (Washington, D.C.: Government Printing Office, 1963), Tables 14 and 17; U.S. Bureau of the Census, *Census of Housing: 1950* (Washington, D.C.: Government Printing Office, 1954).

5. U.S. Bureau of the Census, *Census of Population: 1970*, Table 40; U.S. Bureau of the Census, *Census of Population: 1960*.

6. Jacksonville and Nashville-Davidson have been excluded because their metropolitan-wide governments mean they have either no or almost no suburban rings in terms of census definitions. Albany-Schenectady-Troy has been dropped because some employment data was suppressed. For the 1950-60 period, these SMSAs have been included, but the Fort Lauderdale, Gary-Hammond-East Chicago, Jersey City, Newark, Paterson-Clifton-Passaic, and New York SMSAs have been deleted from the sample; and Los Angeles and Anaheim-Santa Ana-Garden Grove have been combined.

7. Allen D. Manvel, "Land Use in 106 Large Cities," in *Three Land Research Studies*, Research Report No. 12, National Commission on Urban Problems (1968); John H. Niedercorn and Edward F.T. Hearle, "Recent Land Use in 48 Large American Cities," RAND Corp. Memorandum RM-3664-FF (June 1963). The vacant land ratio has been adjusted to an initial value (year at start of time interval) similar to the adjustment made by Niedercorn and Kain, "Econometric Model."

8. D. Farrar and R. Glauber, "Multicollinearity in Regression Analysis," *Review of Economics and Statistics* 49 (February 1967): 92-107. See also J. Johnston, *Econometric Methods* (New York: McGraw-Hill, 2nd ed., 1972), pp. 159-68.

9. Linten, Mields, and Costen, Inc., *A Study of the Problems of Abandoned Housing*, Report to the U.S. Department of Housing and Urban Development (November 1971); *The National Survey of Housing Abandonment* (April 1971); William Lilley, III and Timothy B. Clark, "Federal Programs Spur Abandonment of Housing in Major Cities," *National Journal* (1 January 1972), pp. 26-33.

10. U.S. Bureau of the Census, *U.S. Census of Population: 1970, Number of Inhabitants*, Final Report PC(1) (Washington, D.C.: Government Printing Office, 1971), Tables 6-8.

Chapter 5
Hedonic Price Indexes: An Econometric Analysis
of the Dimensions of the Multifamily Housing Bundle

1. Kelvin Lancaster, *Consumer Demand: A New Approach* (New York: Columbia University Press, 1971).

2. George J. Stigler, *The Theory of Price* (New York: MacMillan, 3rd ed., 1966), pp. 250-52.

3. John F. Kain and John M. Quigley, *Discrimination and a Heterogeneous Housing Stock* (New York: National Bureau of Economic Research, forthcoming), Chapter 2.

4. Zvi Griliches, ed., *Price Indexes and Quality Change* (Cambridge, Mass.: Harvard University Press, 1971), p. 56.

5. Ibid., p. 58.

6. John F. Kain and John M. Quigley, "Measuring the Value of Housing Quality," *Journal of the American Statistical Association* 65 (June 1970), 532-48.

7. William C. Apgar, Jr. and John F. Kain, "Neighborhood Attributes and the Residential Price Geography of Urban Areas" (paper presented at the Winter Meetings of the Econometric Society, Toronto, Ontario, Canada, December 28-30, 1972).

8. J. Johnston, *Econometric Methods*, 2nd ed. (New York: McGraw-Hill, 1972), pp. 155-56.

9. Estimates of the equations in this section using sectorized travel times and nonlinear forms for the travel time and median income variables produced results similar to those summarized in Table 4-2.

10. John F. Kain, "The Journey-to-Work as a Determinant of Residential Location," *Papers and Proceedings of the Regional Science Association* 11 (1962), p. 139.

11. John M. Quigley, "Residential Location with Multiple Workplaces and a Heterogeneous Housing Stock" (Discussion Paper No. 80, Harvard University Program on Regional and Urban Economics, September 1972), pp. 176-81. The maximum value of travel time tried was the wage rate. His analysis of the owner-occupied housing submarket produced no difference in the model's power as the value of travel time was varied.

12. These results parallel John M. Quigley's, "Residential Location," pp. 165-73.

Chapter 6
Suburban Apartments and Restrictive
Zoning Ordinances

1. *Appeal of Girsh*, 263A.2d 395 (Pa., 1970). See also Richard F. Babcock, "Exclusionary Zoning: A Code Phrase for a Notable Legal Struggle" in Louis H.

Masotti and Jeffrey K. Hadden, eds., *The Urbanization of the Suburbs* (Beverly Hills, Calif.: Sage Publications, 1973), pp. 313-28.

2. *In re: Appeal of Kit-Mar Builders.* 268 A.2d 765 (Pa., 1971).

3. John F. Kain, "The Journey-to-Work as a Determinant of Residential Location," in Jon Pynoos, Robert Schafer, and Chester W. Hartman, eds., *Housing Urban America* (Chicago: Aldine, 1973), pp. 211-27; Gregory K. Ingram, John F. Kain and J. Royce Ginn, *The Detroit Prototype of the NBER Urban Simulation Model* (New York: Columbia University Press, 1972). See also, Robert Schafer, "Letter to the Editor," *Journal of the American Institute of Planners* 28 (May 1972): 182. For a discussion of economic theory and zoning ordinances, see William Alonso, *Location and Land Use* (Cambridge, Mass.: Harvard University Press, 1964), pp. 117-25.

4. The zoning data was tabulated and reported by the Metropolitan Area Planning Council in *Residential Zoning in the MAPC Region* (Boston: December 1972).

5. Camp, Dresser, and McKee, *Inventory of Sewer and Water Facilities* (May 1967) as reported in Joseph Flatley, "Housing Construction in the Boston Region," a paper presented to the Urban and Regional Development Seminar in the Department of City and Regional Planning, Harvard University (October 1972).

6. Ibid.

7. Compare *National Land and Investment Company v. Easttown Township*, 419 Pa. 504 (1965) with *Golden v. Town of Ramapo*, 30 N.Y.2d 359 (1972).

8. *Molino v. Borough of Glassboro*, 281 A.2d 401, 405 (N.J., 1971).

Chapter 7
The Future of Apartments in the
Central City

1. *Anatomy of a Metropolis* (New York: Doubleday-Anchor Books, 1962), pp. 162-74.

2. Ibid., p. 173.

3. For an interesting discussion of the conflicts between this goal and the factors influencing the residential location decisions of households, see William Alonso, "The Historic and Structural Theories of Urban Form: Their Implications for Urban Renewal," *Land Economics*, 38 (May 1964), 227-31.

4. Thomas O'Brien and Alexander Ganz, *A Demographic Revolution: The Impact of Office Building and Residential Tower Development in Boston* (Boston: Boston Redevelopment Authority, Research Department, December 1972), pp. 25-36.

5. Ibid., p. 26.

6. U.S. Bureau of the Census, *1970 Census of Population, Fourth Count Summary Tape*, Table 35.

7. Taken from an ad in *The Boston Sunday Globe* (10 June 1973), p. A-71.

8. Ibid.

Chapter 8
Some Additional Policy Implications

1. John R. Meyer and Mahlon R. Straszheim, *Techniques of Transport Planning*, vol. 1 (Washington, D.C.: The Brookings Institution, 1971), pp. 99-136.

2. Gregory K. Ingram, John F. Kain, and Royce Ginn, *The Detroit Prototype of the NBER Urban Simulation Model* (New York: Columbia University Press, 1972); John M. Quigley, "Residential Location with Multiple Workplace and a Heterogeneous Housing Stock," Harvard University Program on Regional and Urban Economics, Discussion Paper No. 80 (September 1972).

3. John R. Meyer, John F. Kain, and Martin Wohl, *The Urban Transportation Problem* (Cambridge, Mass.: Harvard University Press, 1966), p. 364.

4. Ibid., pp. 44-47, 360.

5. *New York Times*, October 23, 1972, p. 35; *New York Times*, July 18, 1973, p. 42.

6. *In Re Appeal of Girsh*, 263A.2d 395 (Pa. 1970).

7. See Max Neutze, *The Suburban Apartment Boom* (Baltimore: Johns Hopkins Press, 1968), p. 44.

8. Philip B. Herr and Associates, *Village House Zoning: An Analysis* (Boston, 1970).

9. Karl Taeuber and Alma Taeuber, *Negroes in Cities* (Chicago: Aldine, 1965); Davis McEntire, *Residence and Race* (Berkeley, California: University of California Press, 1960).

10. John F. Kain and John M. Quigley, "Housing Market Discrimination, Homeownership, and Savings Behavior," *American Economic Review* 62 (June 1972): 263-77.

11. Henry S. Terrell, "The Data on Relative White-Nonwhite Income and Earnings Re-examined," *Journal of Human Resources* 6 (Summer 1971): 386. Copyright by the Regents of the University of Wisconsin. Reprinted with permission.

Index

Index

About the Author

Robert Schafer is Assistant Professor of City and Regional Planning at Harvard University and a Research Associate at the National Bureau of Economic Research. He received the M.S. in physics from Yale University, the J.D. from Harvard Law School, and the Ph.D. in urban planning and economics from Harvard University. He is an editor of *Housing Urban America* (Chicago: Aldine, 1973) and author of *A Place to Live: Housing Policy in the States* (Lexington, Kentucky: Council of State Governments, 1974). Dr. Schafer has contributed articles on housing and other aspects of urban and regional public policy to several journals, including *Land Economics, Public Policy, Journal of Urban Law,* and *Journal of the American Institute of Planners.*